PEI Guide
English for business communications

Graham Collins

Pitman

PITMAN PUBLISHING
128 Long Acre, London, WC2E 9AN

A Division of Longman Group UK Limited

© Graham Collins 1990

First published in Great Britain 1990

British Library Cataloguing in Publication Data
Collins, Graham
  PEI guide to English for business communications.
  1. English language. Business English
  I. Title
  808.066651021

  ISBN 0-273-03199-6

All rights reserved; no part of this publication may be reproduced, stored in a retrieval system, or transmitted in any form or by any other means, electronic, mechanical, photocopying, recording, or otherwise without either the prior written permission of the Publishers or a licence permitting restricted copying in the United Kingdom issued by the Copyright Licensing Agency Ltd, 33–34 Alfred Place, London, WC1E 7DP. This book may not be lent, resold, hired out or otherwise disposed of by way of trade in any form of binding or cover other than that in which it is published, without the prior consent of the Publishers.

Typeset by Tek Art Ltd, Addiscombe, Croydon, Surrey
Printed and bound in Great Britain

Contents

How to use this guide v

Part 1 Elementary 1
Syllabus 2
Elementary checklist 3
Instructions for Part 1 4
1 Reading and comprehension skills 6
2 Vocabulary development by inference 10
3 Types of business letter 13
4 The text of a business letter 19
5 Structuring a letter: paragraphing 22
6 Tone in business letters 25
7 Memorandums 28
8 Telex 31
9 International telegrams and telemessages 34
10 Formal Invitations 37
11 Letters of adjustment or apology 39
12 Letters of complaint 42
13 Letters of explanation 45
14 Sales and promotional letters 48
15 Elementary Examination Questions 51

Part 2 Intermediate 59
Syllabus 60
Intermediate checklist 61
Instructions for Part 2 62
16 Writing a letter from notes: organising and sectioning 63
17 Style and tone 66
18 Writing reports 68
19 Writing a memorandum from notes 71
20 The international telegram (or telex) with a letter of confirmation 74
21 Advertisements 77
22 Testimonials 79
23 Types of personal letter 81
24 Intermediate Examination Questions 84

Part 3 Advanced   95
Syllabus   96
Advanced checklist   97
Instructions for Part 3   98
25 Business letters   99
26 Formal reports   104
27 Concise text (telex/telegram/advertisement)   108
28 Optional questions   109
29 Summary   115
30 Advanced Examination Questions   120
31 Preparing for the English for Business Communications examinations   133

How to use this guide

This guide is designed to provide **practice** and **support** for candidates preparing for entry to the Pitman Elementary, Intermediate and Advanced English for Business Communications examinations.

Effective English for Business Communications requires the continued learning of new information and practising its application to develop new skills. For personal satisfaction and for the benefit of employers, the acquisition of new skills can be proven by passing examinations.

Part I of this guide is designed to be a simple test of the candidates' abilities to compose written correspondence, making effective use of content, presentation, layout, tone and expression.

Part II is designed for those candidates who have already acquired the level of skill dealt with in Part I, which they should demonstrate to their own satisfaction, either by completing some of the Part I final assessments, or by going through the checklist provided on page 3 to ensure that all elements of the Elementary Syllabus have been covered.

Part III requires candidates to build on the skills they have already acquired – again, these can be assessed by going through the checklist on page 65. Candidates will be required to demonstrate a fluent command of English, showing the ability to compose, develop and organise longer and more involved pieces of writing than at either Elementary or Intermediate level.

Each step contains:
- **objectives** which provide a clear outline of the skills or competences to be achieved
- an **example** which clarifies these objectives
- **test your competence** which provides an opportunity to check on the ability to carry out this objective
- **practice from the paper** which provides further realistic practice of the objective taken from a past Pitman Examinations Institute Examination Paper

Each Part of the guide contains a complete past paper at the appropriate level which candidates should attempt before referring to the solution provided. In addition, further practice material is also made available at all levels. These past questions will enable students to appreciate that success in any examination is aided by an awareness of what is commonly called 'examination technique' (see page 141). The guide therefore concludes with recommendations in preparing for examinations.

Finally, a **checklist for candidates**, which may be photocopied, is provided at each level. It is suggested that candidates use these checklists to record their progress and to ensure full coverage of the stated requirements of the examination. If a function or task has been carried out successfully, either with assistance or unaided, then this should be recorded in the appropriate column and the date added.

Note

The author and publishers would like to thank Pitman Examinations Institute for kindly giving permission to reproduce their past examination papers in this guide.

PEI would also like to stress that answers are included for the general guidance of students and in no way do they carry the authority of the examining board.

Part 1 **Elementary**

Syllabus

English for Business Communications

These examinations at Elementary, Intermediate and Advanced levels are intended to test the candidate's skill in using the English language in business correspondence.

Overseas candidates are advised that they should have reached the Intermediate standard of the English for Speakers of Other Languages (ESOL) examination before attempting the English for Business Communications examinations.

At all levels correct layout, tone, spelling and punctuation are of prime importance, as is the ability to use words appropriate to the situation to convey the writer's meaning.

Candidates will be expected to have a background knowledge of office practice; a knowledge of basic office organisations and personnel, a background appreciation of modern office equipment, and staff working conditions.

Exact copying of the questions will be heavily penalised.

Elementary

(Time allowed – 2 hours)
The examination will be in two parts:

Part I – a short objective test, which is compulsory, comprising questions on the correct choice of medium of communication and layout.

Part II – compulsory question (a letter) and a further 3 from a choice of 5.

In Part II candidates will be expected to:

(a) Compose draft letters from notes given dealing with business transactions, including letters of enquiry, complaint, sales letters.
(b) Compose personal letters and formal invitations and replies.
(c) Compose memoranda.
(d) Write international telegrams, telex or other messages on general business matters.

Checklist – Elementary

	Aided	Date	Unaided	Date
1 Reading and comprehension skills Develop vocabulary by reading and consulting a dictionary to aid comprehension.				
2 Vocabulary development by inference Develop vocabulary by making a judgement or conclusion on the basis of existing knowledge.				
3 Types of business letter Recognise the purpose of business letters and the importance of uniform layouts.				
4 The text of a business letter Construct the text of a business letter so that the message is clearly and logically presented.				
5 Structuring a letter: paragraphing Use paragraphs effectively in a letter to break up the message into logical sections.				
6 Tone in business letters Use tone effectively to ensure that the message is delivered in the appropriate manner or style.				
7 Memorandums Recognise the purpose and features of memorandums.				
8 Telex Use the telex as a means of communication and understand its form and purpose.				
9 International telegrams and telemessages				
9.1 Understand how and why to send an international telegram.				
9.2 Understand how and why to send a telemessage.				
10 Formal Invitations Recognise the appropriate style to be used for invitations and ensure that all the relevant details are included.				
11 Letters of adjustment or apology Understand the principles to be applied when writing letters of adjustment or apology and recognise their purpose.				
12 Letters of complaint Understand the principles to be applied when writing letters of complaint.				
13 Letters of explanation Understand the principles to be applied when writing letters of explanation.				
14 Sales and promotional letters Understand the principles to be applied when writing sales and promotional letters.				

Instructions for Part 1

Written communication: four key points

The Pitman examination in English for Business Communications is designed to be a simple test of a candidate's ability to **compose** written correspondence, (the **content** of the answer), and to **present** such correspondence with correct use of **layout**, **tone**, and **expression**. Each of these factors is explained in detail below:-

Content

The content of a letter, memo or other piece of written correspondence consists of the *information that needs to be transferred from one person (the writer) to another (the reader)*. The content needs to be:
- **comprehensive** (it must contain all the information needed)
- **relevant** (it must not contain unnecessary or unimportant information, or anything that is not relevant to the writer's purpose)
- **organised** into a logical sequence, with clear divisions of separate aspects of the subject

Layout

Correct layout depends on:
- the right choice of **medium** (letter, memo, invitation, telex, telemessage, etc.)
- the **correct positioning** of addresses, signatures, headings, etc
- careful **sectioning** and **paragraphing** of material

Tone and style

Tone is defined as 'a particular style in speech or in writing, which expresses or indicates some purpose or feeling.'

The tone and style of written items of business communication is generally official and formal, and does not therefore usually express emotion. But tone may well *convey* attitudes such as **agreement**, **interest**, **caution**, **enquiry**, **satisfaction/dissatisfaction**, etc.)

Expression

Correct expression involves:
- **Accuracy** in grammar, spelling and punctuation
- **clear** and **economic** statement of a message
- the avoidance of common mistakes such as repetition, vagueness and lack of clarity

In this *Guide*, many of the examples given draw attention to the four key aspects listed above. The exercises and questions from past papers in the book are designed to develop your awareness and effective use of these four areas.

As you progress through the *Guide*, you should develop the habit of reading an examination question and planning your answer by thinking out the needs of each area (*content, layout, tone, expression*) in turn.

If you consider these **four key factors** each time you start a question, you will be sure to cover all the issues involved. You will also develop a methodical and effective approach to the planning and production of your written communication.

THE FOUR KEY FACTORS in WRITTEN COMMUNICATION

CONTENT	LAYOUT
TONE/STYLE	EXPRESSION

Think in terms of these **four key issues** *every time* you work through an exercise in this Exam Guide.

1 Reading and comprehension skills

Develop vocabulary by reading and consulting a dictionary to aid comprehension.

Reading is a basic skill which is fundamental in business and commercial activity. It is impossible to work successfully in a modern organisation, especially an office, without well developed reading comprehension skills.

Reading comprehension involves the ability to read and understand a piece of writing. In the PEI English for Business Communication examination at Elementary level, reading skill is tested with a compulsory question at the beginning of the paper. To complete the question, you will be required to fill gaps in a passage of writing, by selecting appropriate words from a list at the foot of the page. The exercise demands good *vocabulary skills*.

A person's vocabulary consists of the range of words they are able to understand and use. An individual with an extensive vocabulary will be able to read, think, speak and write more effectively and usefully than one with a limited vocabulary.

A vocabulary is developed by reading, and by talking and working with others. Many fields of knowledge have their own specialised vocabularies. For example, the words *plaintiff, counsel, indenture, witness* and *liability* are all drawn from the vocabulary of the law while the words megabyte, modem and software are all drawn from the area of computing.

By reading, talking and learning in these areas, the full meaning of *specialised* vocabulary will become clear to you. Once it is clear, your ability to think and work in the specialist area of knowledge concerned becomes much greater and more effective.

Pitman Examination Institute papers in English for Business Communication at Elementary level include a compulsory reading question because the ability to read and use vocabulary is so essential in business life at all levels.

The vocabulary and subject matter used in the reading exercises are always drawn from the area of Office and Commercial Studies. So in order to develop a wide vocabulary and reading skills, you are recommended to read books and periodicals (magazines).

On this subject. Magazines such as *Business Education Today* will be helpful.

You can develop your vocabulary by encountering new words and learning their meanings. One way in which meaning can be learned is by using a dictionary, which explains the meaning of new items of vocabulary. The process of developing and expanding vocabulary often operates as a simple, three-stage process:

READ PASSAGE
↓
ENCOUNTER NEW VOCABULARY ITEM
↓
OVERCOME DIFFICULTY OF NEW VOCABULARY ITEM BY DICTIONARY EXPLANATION

As a result you will understand the passage more easily and increase your vocabulary. Of course, difficulties caused by new vocabulary may be overcome without recourse to a dictionary. A simple explanation of the meaning of a word from a friend or teacher may solve the difficulty.

Test your competence

Read through the following passage. If you encounter any unfamiliar words, make a list of them. Then check their meanings in a dictionary.

SECRETARY OF THE FUTURE

In the UK alone there are some 10 million office workers occupying 400,000 offices, who now account for about 40% of the entire workforce. Indeed, social and economic historians refer to ours as the 'post-industrial information society', in which the processing of all kinds of information – from share prices to the availability of various types of motor car, hot off the production line – is zapped almost instantaneously around the world.

Explosive growth

To cope with the explosive growth of information exchange and the value top management places upon it in keeping ahead of competitors, managers in all kinds of offices, from R&D to Marketing, are having to rethink strategies from basic. How should they organise what staff to interact with what type of equipment, in order to obtain, process, and distribute the information needed to keep their organisation in the running?

The member of staff with a central role to play in this IT-driven restructuring is, of course, the secretary, in the various roles of personal assistant, private, personal or executive secretary, since it is the secretary in most offices who is most intimately occupied with the increasingly complex business of information processing.

The IT-based electronic office revolution – first termed as such in the late 1970s in the USA – has now gained such a momentum in the UK that secretarial posts are currently being given a new nomenclature in advertisements, which acknowledges the significant changes and extensions in their roles. Secretarial posts are now being offered as 'Information Assistant' or 'Information Services Officer', and a new career route is being opened up into posts such as 'Communications Manager' or 'Information Services Co-ordinator'.

Computerisation
The driving force of such radical organisational and structural change has been the widespread introduction of microprocessor-driven systems and equipment. The Intel Corporation of the USA marketed the first commercially available microprocessor, or silicon chip, in 1971. In a short eighteen years it has transformed business practice and changed the fact of cultures and societies across the world.

Nowhere has the microprocessor had more impact than in today's private and public sector offices.

Extracted from *Secretarial Procedures in the Electronic Office* by Desmond Evans, Pitman Publishing 1989

Practice from the paper

Now attempt the following examination question which is based on an understanding of business vocabulary.

Using the list of words given below, fill in the blank spaces in this passage.

sending	year	signature	firm	telegraphic
month	dictated	typed	name	spelling
accurate	punctuation	faithfully	queries	letter
full	salutation	complimentary	address	telex

A firm's first impression of another firm may be from a .... received from it. It is very important that the typing is neat and .... and that .... and .... are correct. The reference on a letter indicates who has .... and .... the letter and it helps when any .... have to be looked into at a later date. Business letters always have the .... and .... of the firm .... the letter printed at the top. There may also be a .... address and .... number. The date is always written in ...., the order usually being day, ..., ... Dear Sir or Dear Mr Smith is known as the .... and Yours faithfully or Yours sincerely is called the .... close. It is important that the correct complimentary close is used. If the letter begins Dear Sir it should end Yours .... After the complimentary close it is usual to type the name of the .... A suitable space is then left for .... Under the signature the name of the person signing the letter is typed.

8 English for business communications

Check your success

The words appeared in the following order. Tick the boxes if you got the words right.

Letter	☐	Telegraphic	☐
Accurate	☐	Telex	☐
Spelling *or* Punctuation	☐	Full	☐
Punctuation *or* Spelling	☐	Month	☐
Dictated	☐	Year	☐
Typed	☐	Salutation	☐
Queries	☐	Complimentary	☐
Name	☐	Faithfully	☐
Address	☐	Firm	☐
Sending	☐	Signature	☐

2 Vocabulary development by inference

Develop vocabulary by making a judgement or conclusion on the basis of existing knowledge.

You have already learned that reading skills and vocabulary can be developed by the use of a dictionary.

However, the dictionary has its limitations. It is not always there when it is needed; often, it is necessary to read a piece of writing with difficult vocabulary when no dictionary is available.

In addition, dictionary use can make reading slow. Frequent interruptions of reading to consult a dictionary can break the flow of reading, and damage your concentration and understanding.

Because of these limitations, you are advised to use the dictionary sparingly, turning to consult it only when you are really unsure of the meaning of a word. Readers will also try to **infer** the meaning of a word. To infer means *to make a judgement or conclusion on the basis of existing knowledge*. You can infer the meaning of new vocabulary by judging the general sense of the passage, and by looking at the **context** of words surrounding the new item of vocabulary. Obviously, this skill is particularly important in an examination, where dictionaries are not available.

Example

The word 'malleable' in the following sentence is an unusual and perhaps difficult word for the general reader.

'The clay can be cut, hammered or even moulded by hand into various shapes. Because it is so **malleable**, it is ideal for young children who are learning how to use both their hands and simple tools to make a variety of shapes.'

You can **infer** that 'malleable' means easy to bend or press into various shapes, without breaking.

The following diagram shows how you can develop and extend your vocabulary.

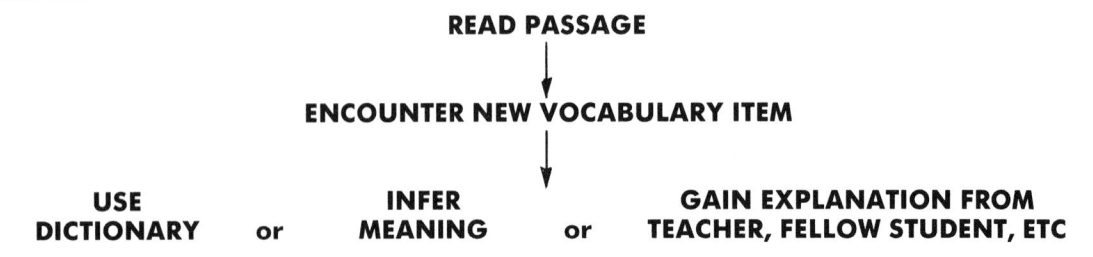

10 English for business communications

Test your competence

Try to infer the meaning of the words that appear in **bold** in the following passage. Note down your inference on the meaning, and then check the meaning in a dictionary, if necessary.

National Vocational Qualifications are awarded to people who prove that they can perform **competently** in employment – as opposed to traditional **vocational** qualifications which are given for completion of a **formal** course. To gain such qualifications, participants **accumulate** units of competence over a period of time. As Professor Thompson says in his statement:
   'It **requires** those in employment to **define** the **outcomes** needed, and those in education to decide what type of learning is required.'
Adapted from *Business Education Today*, March 1989

Practice from the paper

Test your ability to infer vocabulary by doing the questions without a dictionary.

Using the list of words given below fill in the blank spaces in this passage.

typewritten	advertisement	paragraphs	referees
handwritten	first	formally	education
employed	examination	work	testimonials
originals	permission	copies	interview
confirming	source	employer	references

A letter of application is usually your .... introduction to a prospective .... Your letter should be .... unless the .... calls for a .... letter. Plan the letter carefully, especially the arrangement of .... Refer to the .... of the advertisement and apply .... for the post. Give full details of your .... and any .... successes. If you have been .... previously give any information that may be of help. For example, give details of the .... you did. If the advertisement asks for it, give the names and addresses of .... or enclose copies of .... These should be neatly typed .... of the originals. Never send the .... which can be produced later if required. When .... are to be given you should obtain your referees' .... to use their names. In your application you should always include a statement showing your willingness to attend for .... If you are invited for an interview be sure to reply at once, ... that you will be able to attend.

Vocabulary development by inference

Using the words supplied below fill in the blank spaces.

memoranda	letters	salutation	reference	to
from	memo	typed	printed	A5
internal	subject	ref	recipient	complimentary
sender	important	memorandum	date	close
				layout

Within a business .... are the equivalent of .... sent to people outside. They are in fact .... correspondence. They are usually written or .... on specially .... forms which are often of .... size. Memoranda should be as short as possible. There are many variations in the .... of a memorandum but there are some .... items that must appear. The word .... sometimes abbreviated to .... always appears at the top of the form. The space where the names and titles of the .... and .... are to be written are indicated by the words .... and .... The word .... is followed by the space in which the date is written. If a .... is included it is written in the space indicated by the abbreviation .... The word .... indicates that a title or heading is needed. As memoranda are used for internal correspondence there is no need for a .... or ....

Check your success

Did you use these words, in the correct order?

1 First	6 Paragraphs	11 Employed	16 Originals
2 Employer	7 Source	12 Work	17 References
3 Typewritten	8 Formally	13 Referees	18 Permission
4 Advertisement	9 Education	14 Testimonials	19 Interview
5 Handwritten	10 Examination	15 Copied	20 Confirming

1 Memorandum	6 A5	11 Sender	16 Reference
2 Letters	7 Layout	12 Recipient	17 Ref
3 Internal	8 Important	13 To	18 Subject
4 Typed	9 Memorandum	14 From	19 Salutation
5 Printed	10 Memo	15 Date	20 Complimentary Close

12 English for business communications

3 Types of business letter

Recognise the purpose of business letters and the importance of uniform layouts.

Letters have been a fundamental means of communication and negotiation in business life for hundreds of years. Many different types of business letters have evolved to serve a variety of purposes. The most common and important types are illustrated in this guide. A letter may
- express a simple enquiry (letter of enquiry)
- propose a business arrangement, project or venture (letter of proposal)
- confirm an agreement or arrangement that has been made, either by word of mouth or by telex or telegram (letter of confirmation)
- express a complaint, and seek remedial action (letter of complaint)
- explain or notify a change in previous arrangements or operations (letter of adjustment)

Many of these types of letter are dealt with fully in Units 11–14.

Whatever the particular purpose of a business letter, it will show some common aspects with other business letters. It is always an ambassador or representative for its company, and will therefore show the following features:
- **a letterhead** with name, address, and telephone number of the organisation sending the letter
- the **date** of writing
- the **addressee** – the name, title and address of the recipient.
- **a subject heading** – a title before the text of the letter indicating the main subject of the letter.
- **clear wording** and **clearly sectioned** (paragraphed) layout
- **salutation** and **subscription** as appropriate.

Example

Acme Sports Limited
55 The Crescent
Knowsley
Lancashire L17 5RG Tel: (067) 576839

15 November 19–

Mr J Tobias
6 The Laurels
Knowsley LANCS

Dear Mr Tobias

SETS OF FOOTBALL KIT

I am writing to confirm information as given earlier today.

We will be pleased to supply a set of 12 adult football kits, each set comprising one orange shirt, one pair of white shorts and one pair of white socks, at a price of £135.00 with free delivery.

If purchased separately, individual sets of kit are priced at £16.00 per set.

The kit is in stock, and can be supplied immediately on our receipt of your order and payment.

Yours sincerely

J Prandu
Manager

The features of letters will now be explained.

Date

It is important to date every letter as letters are often filed and kept on permanent record. Letters may also form a **sequence** of items of communication. An individual letter may be part of an involved process of negotiation between a number of organisations and individuals. The date may appear in the top right hand corner of a letter, below the address of the sender or on the left above the address of the recipient. The date may be expressed in longhand form, as 23 August 19– or 23rd August 19–. Alternatively it may be in number form, with a series of numbers indicating day, month and year: 23.8.19–.

Test your competence

In the following table, some dates are expressed longhand and others in number. Fill in the missing spaces.

Longhand	Number
15 September 1989	....
....	11.3.1993
8 August 1987	....
....	25.11.1986
9 May 1983	....
....	4.10.1992
26 February 1990	....
....	12.12.1991

Reference A letter may contain a reference coding from the writer. This will consist of the writer's initials, followed by the typist's initials and sometimes by a filing code. A letter written by Victor Ujoma and typed by Lillian Bays, which is from file 453.J will therefore include the reference VU/LB/453J.

Addressee Business letters always carry two addresses at the top of the letter — the address of the writer, and the name and address of the recipient, or addressee.

This is because copies of letters are kept by the sending organisation, as a record of the business relationship with the recipient company or person.

Salutation The salutation is the greeting phrase which opens the letter. It is customary to open a letter with the salutation

> Dear Sir *or* Dear Sir or Madam

if the letter is to an individual you have not previously met.

> Dear Sirs

to a group or company you have not previously met.

> Dear Mr Davidson or Dear Mrs Beale etc.

to individuals you *have* previously met or dealt with.

It is important to remember that the principal words of a salutation open with capital letters.

Subject heading This is usually written in block letters, and often underlined. It is placed after the salutation, and prior to the main body of the letter. It announces the principal purpose or subject of the letter.

Subscription The subscription is used when a letter is 'signed off'. It is usual to close a letter with

> Yours faithfully

if you have not previously met the recipient or

>   Yours sincerely

if you have met the recipient

Other forms of subscription, such as 'Kindest regards' may be used if the relationship between writer and recipient is well established.
Notice that only the word 'Yours' in the subscription carries a capital letter: words such as 'faithfully' or 'sincerely' do not.
These six points of theory are important aspects of letter layout and presentation.

Test your competence

This letter is incorrectly set out. List the errors in its layout, then rewrite the letter improving its layout and inventing further details as necessary.

Task Industries
5 Morton Vale
London SE13

To: Bown and Co

Dear Bown and Co

We have not yet received the stationery ordered and paid for in our previous letter. Please could you despatch this order urgently, or contact us with an explanation.

Yours

S. Green

Task Industries

Check your success

Did you notice:

Task Industries gives no telephone number ☐

The letter is not dated ☐

The letter carries no reference number ☐

The addressee is incompletely written ☐

There is no subject heading ☐

The subscription is incomplete ☐

The letter is not signed by an individual at Task Industries? ☐

16   English for business communications

A more correct version would be like this:

                                                Task Industries
                                                    Head Office
                                                    5 Morton Vale
                                                 London SE13 2VG

                                                  Tel: 071 692 8814

Our ref: DH/PL

Mr J Patel
Orders Dept
Bown and Co
5 Longdale Avenue
London SW11 5PZ   18 July 19-

Dear Mr Patel

                      <u>OVERDUE STATIONERY ORDER</u>

We have not yet received the stationery ordered and paid for in our letter of 9 June 19-.

Please could you despatch this order urgently, or contact me with an explanation on the above telephone number. I look forward to hearing from you shortly.

Yours sincerely

Donald Harna

Donald Harma
Buying Dept

This letter is correctly laid out and is likely to gain a prompt response from the recipient, who has all the details required.

It should now be clear that the layout of a letter is an important factor in correct and effective communication by letter.

Practice from the paper: You work for the secretary to the Headmaster, Mr R Carter, Elmpark Comprehensive School, Highwood Chase, Brighton, BR8 54U. Draft a letter to Mrs Janet Blackwood, a former pupil of the school, who has recently returned from three years working in schools in Nigeria. She has written a book about her experiences and has become a local celebrity. Mr Carter would like her to talk about her work at the Senior Prizegiving on Friday, 11 December at 2.30 pm, and to present the prizes to the senior pupils. After the Prizegiving there will be an opportunity for informal chat and refreshments. Mrs Blackwood lives at Flat 32, Grove Court, Brighton, BR9 76T. The letter is for Mr Carter's signature. His reference is RC/HJ.

Types of business letter

Check your success

Did your letter have

- Your address in full in the top right-hand corner ☐
- The addressee's name (Mrs Janet Blockwood) and address on the left ☐
- The date ☐
- The reference ☐
- A salutation 'Dear Mrs Blockwood' ☐
- A complimentary close ☐
- All necessary details? ☐

4 The text of a business letter

Construct the text of a business letter so that the message is clearly and logically presented.

The main text of a business letter is the continuous written message enclosed between the salutation and the subscription.

It is important that the **text** of the letter is skilfully and carefully constructed. The following principles and examples are guidelines for the construction of the text of letters:
- the main topic of the letter should feature in the subject heading.
- the opening paragraph should introduce the topic of the letter. Where there has been previous correspondence on the topic, this should be referred to, with the appropriate date.
- the letter should present information in a clearly sequenced, easily understandable way, with all necessary details clearly included.
- paragraphs should be used to divide differing areas of the topic into a logical and manageable sequence.
- the letter's closing paragraph should state any action that is necessary on the part of either the sender or the recipient of the letter.

Example

```
                                    BJS Yachts Ltd
                                    The Marina
                                    Southampton
                                    Hants SO5 3JG

                                    Tel: 064 47762

Our ref:   JB/CF


Welcome Cars Ltd
Ringway Airport
Manchester MU7 5PD

Dear Sirs

            CHAIRMAN'S VISIT TO MANCHESTER 04.05.-

I write regarding our booking, confirmed in your letter of
28.3.-, for one of your cars to transport our Chairman, Mr P D
Chan, from the airport to the Hotel Picadilly, Manchester.

Mr Chan has had to change his travel arrangements.  The new
arrangements are as follows:

1   Mr Chan will now arrive at Manchester on British Airways flight
BA 101, departing London Heathrow at 14.00 hours on 4 May, due at
Manchester at 14.50 hours.
```

2. Mr Chan will now be travelling alone. As he does not drive, he will require a chauffeured car to the hotel.

We would be glad if you could confirm your receipt of this letter, and also confirm that arrangements are in hand.

We look forward to hearing from you.

Yours faithfully

J. Bland

J BLAND
Chairman's Secretary

In this example, the text of the letter opens by introducing the topic and referring to previous correspondence.

The text explains and concludes the topic suitably, and *specifies* important details, such as the time of arrival, and the need for a driver.

The *conclusion* not only rounds off the message – it also contains a request for further correspondence, in the form of a confirmation.

Test your competence

You are the Stores Supervisor of COOLSIP LTD, Unit Four, Industrial Estate, Pyhurst, Lincs L14 2JG, a manufacturer of soft drinks, which are sold in bottles and cans. You receive a regular monthly order of 40 000 plastic bottle caps (24 millimetres diameter) from BALDOCK LTD, Arthur Lane, Grantham, Lincs, GR5 8DG.

The monthly delivery due for June was 60 000 caps, to cope with high orders caused by hot summer weather. When you receive the order, there are only 40 000. Of these, 10 000 are only 20 millimetres in diameter, and will not fit COOLSIP bottles.

Write a letter to the Sales Department of Baldock Ltd, addressed to Mrs Carlita Browning, Sales Director. Explain the problem, including all necessary details, and request urgent action.

Check your success

Did the subject heading refer to *errors in June order*, or *errors in delivery*? ☐

Did the opening establish that the delivery was a regular monthly one, but that an error had been made in the case of the June delivery? ☐

Did the mid section of the letter explain:

that the order was for more caps than usual? ☐

that the wrong number of caps were delivered? ☐

that some caps of the wrong size were delivered? ☐

Did the letter *conclude* by politely and firmly insisting on prompt correction of the errors? (It could also point out the difficulties for

COOLSIP LTD that would follow if Baldock Ltd did not promptly correct their mistakes.) ☐

Practice from the paper

A wholesale firm from whom you buy goods, John Little & Sons, 21 High Street, Newtown, NS1 3BW has invited you to send two representatives to their Centenary celebrations next month. Reply by letter stating that Mr John Green, the Sales Manager and Miss Nancy Wright, the Buyer, will attend. Send your congratulations and express your firm's thanks for the excellent service to you at all times. You work for Metal Box Sundries Ltd, Grey Street, Manchester, M2 4XJ and Charles Kildare, Chief Administrative Officer will sign the letter.

Check your success

Did your letter have

    your address in full at the top right hand corner ☐

    the addressee's name and address on the left ☐

    the date ☐

    the reference ☐

    the correct salutation at the end? ☐

Did the body of the letter express clearly

    who would be attending the celebrations ☐

    suitable congratulations/thanks? ☐

5 Structuring a letter: paragraphing

Use paragraphs effectively in a letter to break up the message into logical sections.

Structuring a letter means putting it together in a clear, suitable and effective way. This generally involves breaking the message into **sections**, and writing a **paragraph** in the body of the letter for each section.

A **paragraph** is a unit of writing, usually consisting of several sentences, which explains or develops one point or topic. If the message in the letter is very simple, some letters will need to consist of only a single paragraph.

Example

```
                                World Magazine
                                  PO Box 11
                                 London WC1

                              Tel: 071 463 4685

Ref DW/VG

Mr J Chalmers
8 Duncan Street                                      23 January 19-
Glasgow


Dear Sir

                           ANNUAL SUBSCRIPTION

Would you please note that your annual subscription is due for
renewal on the first day of next month.  An invoice and addressed
envelope is enclosed for your convenience.

Yours faithfully


David Weston


DAVID WESTON
Subscriptions Manager
```

However, many letters are more involved than this and will need a number of paragraphs. As we discussed earlier in the section on the text of a business letter, at least three sections will often be included: an **introductory** sentence or paragraph, a more detailed **mid-section** and a **conclusion**.

English for business communications

Therefore, while letters will often have at least three paragraphs, if the subject matter is involved, and necessitates a prolonged mid-section, then more paragraphs will be needed.

Test your competence

You are Personal Assistant to Mrs Marian Ohsan, Finance Director of Appleyard Computers Ltd, 5 The Headway, Coventry CO2 8PD. You find the following note on your desk:

Please draft a letter (to be ready for my signature by 3 pm today) to go to Arden Vehicles Ltd in London Road. Advise them that we want to renew our service agreement on our 4 Ford Transit vans for another year, but with each van being fully serviced every 10 000 miles, not every 12 000 as this year. Ask them to give us a written price quote for the new arrangement.

Also, get them to quote a price for supplying and fitting two way radio systems into the vans, with a two way unit here, so that we can keep in touch with all our delivery drivers. We need all these quotes for the Board of Directors meeting, so stress the urgency of the request.

Thanks,
Marian

Check your success

Did your letter have: a subject heading, such as 'vehicle leasing' or similar? ☐

Did you include an *introductory* paragraph, explaining that Appleyard Computers do want to renew their leasing agreement, but are interested in considering some changes? ☐

Did you include a paragraph in the body of the letter to explain the two changes, (servicing after fewer miles, and the installation of two way radio)? ☐

Did your letter end with a concluding paragraph, requesting detailed quotes by letter, and stressing urgency? ☐

Practice from the paper

You are applying for a post as a junior shorthand-typist and would like your former headmistress, Mrs B Calender of the High School for Girls, Queenstown, Birmingham, B12 3LN to support your application. Write to her asking if she would send you a testimonial as to your record at school both academically and socially.

Structuring a letter: paragraphing 23

Worked example

24 Rainsborough Street
Birmingham B11 8YH

24 April 19

Mrs B Calender
Headteacher
The High School for Girls
Queenstown
Birmingham B12 3LN

Dear Mrs Calender

<u>JOB APPLICATION</u>

You may remember that I left Queenstown last Summer after a very happy time there as a pupil. Since leaving, I have done a course in typing at the Technical College, and I have now decided to apply for a job with Bilston and Forbes, an engineering company here in Birmingham. I am writing to ask you if you would be kind enough to provide me with a testimonial.

As you will see from the job advertisement which I enclose, the post is suitable for a junior shorthand typist who can deal with some simple telephone and reception duties. You may remember that I gained a distinction in the Office Practice class at school, and I feel that this part of my education at Queenstown may be helpful and relevant.

I am very grateful for any help that you may be able to give, and remember the staff and my school friends from Queenstown with some happiness. I do hope to meet you again before too long, and to receive a testimonial from you in the near future.

Yours sincerely

Bindu Vithlani

Bindu Vithlani

Check your success

Did your letter have

- The sender's address ☐
- The date ☐
- A personalised salutation (Dear Mrs Calender) ☐
- An introductory paragraph (explaining your application) ☐
- A main paragraph (requesting a testimonial) ☐
- A concluding paragraph (with a courteous close) ☐
- A suitable subscription (Yours sincerely)? ☐

English for business communications

6 Tone in business letters

Use tone effectively to ensure that the message is delivered in the appropriate manner or style.

Tone is extremely important in business communication as it is often a strong influence on the attitude of the listener or reader. It can be defined as *the manner or style in which a message is delivered*. Frequently, tone is an indicator of the underlying attitude or mood of the sender of the message.

Management of tone is a vital and difficult aspect of business communication. It is easy to project an unhelpful, uncooperative attitude if the tone of business communication is too formal or distant. Equally, however, business communication is a formal and official procedure, and tone needs to be suitably serious.

Later in the book, the tone of particular types of letter, such as sales letters and letters of complaint, will be examined. But first, it is useful to establish some general principles for the tone of business letters.

A business letter should:
- be official and reasonably formal, unless it is written between long established friends or business associates
- avoid the expression of undue emotion or feeling
- project an image of precision, efficiency and control.

Example

Look at the following letter written by the owner of a café to the manufacturer of a refrigerator.

The Cup and Saucer
52 Kings Highway, Cheltenham Glos CH1 4EX   Tel: 0803 72415

```
Standard Refrigeration Ltd
Industrial Park
East Vale
Nottingham NO3 2HC

Dear Sirs

          STANDARD P3 REFRIGERATOR

I placed an order for one of the above refrigerators on 10 February
this year.  I was advised that there was free delivery, guaranteed
to be within 14 days, if I paid in advance, which I did.

The refrigerator was in fact delivered on 11 March, rather later
```

than promised. I was prepared to overlook this, but as you know, the refrigerator proved faulty, and was returned to you on March 26th.

You have neither provided a replacement, nor indicated a date for delivery and installation of the repaired refrigerator.

The absence of a large refrigerator is causing both waste of food and a restriction in the menu I can offer.

Would you please investigate this matter urgently and let me have your immediate comments by letter or telephone.

Yours sincerely,

Maria Costello

Maria Costello (Miss)
Proprietor

This letter is written with an appropriate and well controlled tone. The writer clearly expresses her dissatisfaction, but is never discourteous. She also explains what she would like to be done in a clear, inoffensive way.

The letter meets the standard requirements for tone in business correspondence. It is

- official and formal
- controlled
- unemotional

Test your competence

Draft a letter in response to one of the following problems. Invent details, including names and addresses, as necessary.

1 You work in the Accounts Department of DIXMAN'S, a high street hi-fi and camera store. One of your customers has failed to make a monthly payment instalment of £23.50 on a video camera he is buying from you. Write him a letter, pointing out the missed instalment and asking him to make the payment as soon as possible.

Worked example

Dixmans Ltd
156–159 The Reddings
Boxley PH5 3RT

Tel: (0566) 48573

Mr J H Radley
44 Upland Avenue
Boxley PR3 6HJ

Dear Mr Radley

OVERDUE INSTALMENT: ACCOUNT NO:4/1138

We are writing to advise you that a monthly payment of £23.50, in connection with your purchase of a Zoomstar Video Camera from this branch on 18 March 19–, has not been made. The payment was due on 15 October.

26 English for business communications

We are sure that this was an oversight, but would be glad if you
could arrange for an immediate payment to clear the arrears. We
would advise you that a payment of £47.00 on the 15th of this month
will be an acceptable way to clear the arrears, and at the same time
keep your account up to date.

Please do not hesitate to contact me by telephone if there is any
need to discuss this matter further.

Yours sincerely

Marina Damon

Marina Damon
Branch Accounts Manager

---

2 Your company, Mercury Vending Ltd., leases a small car park of five parking spaces at the foot of the office block you share with another, much bigger company. Despite notices that state that it is a private parking area, some of your spaces are frequently occupied by executives in the larger company, Rattan Finance Ltd. Write a letter to the Managing Director of Rattan Finance in which you point out the problem, and ask him to ensure that his staff stop using your private car park.

Practice from the paper

Write a letter from Mr J Barnard, Sales Manager, Vellum Paper Company, Blackwater Lane, Aberdeen, A12 3BW, to Mr D Ager, Purchasing Manager, Pilgrim Books, Bailey Road, Inverness, INZ 9XB, telling him that Mr Smithson, who had been the representative for his area, has had to retire early owing to ill health. Within a few days his replacement, Mr J Green, will be calling on his company. Tell him that you have a special offer at the moment for bulk orders and that Mr Green will have further details regarding this. Thank them for their custom in the past and express hope that it may long continue. Mr Barnard's reference is JB/FP.

Check your success

Is your letter correctly set out, with

    address ☐

    addressee ☐

    reference ☐

    subject heading? ☐

Does your letter express regrets at Mr Smithson's retirement by using a word like 'unfortunately' or 'alas'? ☐

Does the tone of your letter express gratitude for past orders? ☐

Does the tone of your letter encourage further orders? ☐

Does the tone of your letter remain suitably serious and formal throughout? ☐

7 Memorandums

Recognise the purpose and features of memorandums.

The business letter is the single most important means of communication between commercial and industrial organisations. It has the benefit of providing an inexpensive, permanent record of communication between organisations.

Several other forms of written communication are commonly used in business. These include the memorandum (memo), facsimile transmission (fax), telex, telemessage (in the UK) and international telegram.

The memorandum, or memo as it is frequently called, is used for communication within an organisation. A memo provides written contact for instructions, advice, enquiries and notification between different individuals or departments within the same organisation. The memo has a simpler layout than a letter with the following key aspects:

- at the head of the page, three simple notes record **to** whom the memo is sent, who it is **from**, and the **date** of writing. If the memo requires an urgent response, then the **time** of writing may accompany the date.
- a subject heading, which may be above the text of the memo, as in a business letter, or may follow the heading '**re**' (regarding) on the memo itself.
- The signature or initials of the sender may accompany the message.

Example

<u>MEMORANDUM</u>

TO: Transport Manager
FROM: Accounts Department   DATE: 11.4.19-

RE: <u>FUEL BILLS</u>

You have not yet given us receipts for fuel bought by the fleet drivers during March.

This omission is delaying end of year financial accounts. Please supply the receipts by the end of this week, at the latest!

A number of features about the memo are different from the letter.
- a memo carries no salutation or subscription
- the wording of a memo is more direct and often more informal than

the wording of a letter. A memo may even consist of notes and include abbreviations.
- the signatory of a memo does not always need to include their job title, as this communication is intended for a colleague within the same organisation.
- though neither the language nor content of a memo need be as formal as those of a letter, they do need to be clear, and to include all necessary details.

Test your competence

Write a memo to deal with each of the following problems:

1 You are the Personnel Manager of an engineering company employing 120 engineers. You are trying to plan summer holiday arrangements for the firm which will keep at least 80 engineers at work during the peak summer months of July and August. The Managing Director has asked you to encourage staff to take holiday outside these dates wherever possible.

Write a memo to all the engineers explaining the position and ask them to notify you of their first and second choice for their two-week holiday.

2 As Finance Director of a large travel agent with 18 branches, you have just started selling holidays to the new destinations of Bali and Romania. Bookings for each of these centres have been poor. Write a memo to the manager of each branch, asking whether brochures on these holidays are sufficiently well displayed, and whether branches are doing enough to sell holidays to these destinations. Finally, announce an offer of a £50 cash bonus to any branch manager who can sell more than 10 holidays to each destination in any month.

3 You are Chief Safety Officer in a large oil refinery. Write a memo to all section managers reminding them of the need to carry out annual checks on all their fire equipment (hoses, extinguishers, sprinkler systems), and offer to assist with these checks. Explain that fire drills are planned for the following week, and remind managers of their duty to train their own staff in fire drill procedures.

Practice from the paper

Write a memorandum from the Manager of the Supersave Food Store to all junior employees, informing them that a special course is being arranged at Head Office in Cambridge to train junior staff who have not previously spent time at the store's check-out tills. It will be held from 10 – 14 May. All expenses will be paid by the Company. All people wishing to attend should give their names to the Staff Training Officer by the end of the week.

Check your success

Does your memo have the following:

Space for name of sender (... from ....)? ☐

Space for name of recipients (... to ...)? ☐

Date? ☐

Subject heading? ☐

Signature or initials? ☐

Clear, brief wording and explanation? ☐

8 Telex

Use the telex as a means of communication and understand its form and purpose.

A telex machine is a keyboard linked to a telephone line. A telex message can be written and checked, and then sent through a telephone line to print out on a receiving telex machine anywhere in the world.

Telex therefore provides a means of extremely speedy written communication between business addresses across the world. Telex messages can be used to issue instructions, confirm agreements, and to transfer money from one bank to another, and across international boundaries.

Although telex messages are often important in formalising agreements between individuals and companies, they are set out more simply than business letters.

When sending a telex, instead of listing the address, identify yourself by listing your answerback code (a telex number, usually with an abbreviated code to represent the name of your company, and perhaps the country of origin. For example, the telex code of Capital Intelligence Ltd of Cyprus is 3379 CAPINTL CY). This coding is added automatically by a telex machine to any message that is sent.

The text of a telex message is frequently abbreviated, in order to control line charges. For example, look at the following telex sent from Apex Turbines Ltd of the UK to Mediterranean Yachts Ltd of Limassol, Cyprus. The form of the message is *briefer* and *simpler* than that of a letter. There is no subject heading, no full listing of address and addressee, and the text is expressed in briefer language than is used in a letter.

Example

```
90-01-18  09:54
Msg 291 Title: AW1

627491 APEX G          -    TELEX NUMBER AND ANSWERBACK CODE OF SENDER

2668 MEDYAT CY         -    TELEX NUMBER AND ANSWERBACK CODE OF RECEIVER.

FROM:  CLIVE TAYLOR, SALES MANAGER.
TO:    ACCOUNTS DEPT.
RE:    DIESEL ENGINE ENQUIRY.

RE.  YOUR ENQUIRY DIESEL ENGINES TYPE 54/B.  WE CONFIRM PRICE AT
U.K. £1,400.00 PER ENGINE EX WORKS.  DISCOUNT OF 20% APPLICABLE TO
TOTAL OF ALL ORDERS EXCEEDING SIX ENGINES.  STOCKS CURRENTLY GOOD.
WE CAN DESPATCH WITHIN 48 HOURS OF CONFIRMED ORDER.  PLEASE NOTE
DESPATCH COSTS OF U.K. £350.00 PER ENGINE, AND OUR PAYMENT TERMS OF
50% IN ADVANCE, BALANCE ON DELIVERY TO YOU IN CYPRUS.  PLEASE
NOTIFY YOUR ORDER ASAP.  REGARDS, CLIVE TAYLOR.

627491 APEX G              DATE AND TIME   27.04.90   16.17
```

Test your competence

Set out the following telexes as clearly as you can. Include all the important information, but be more economical in wording than you would be in a letter.

1 Set out a telex from Pinnacle Computers Ltd in the United Kingdom (Telex 21842 PICOM G) to United Fruit Company, Lagos Nigeria (Telex 57331 UNFCOM NG) stating that Mr G Farmer, Maintenance Engineer, will arrive in Lagos on flight no BA734 from London Heathrow, scheduled to arrive at 17.50 local time on September 22 19—. Mr Farmer will stay at the Lagos International Hotel and will supervise the maintenance of United Fruit's computer system as agreed from 23–25 September inclusive.

2 Set out a telex from EUREXPORT LTD (37249 EUREX G) in the UK to AUTOSTRADA spa, TURIN ITALY (telex 51126 AUTO I) confirming that five Ford Escort XR3i cars have been exported by transporter from Dover on 11.5.—, and are due to arrive by transporter in Turin on 15.5.—.

3 Send a telex from Hill Govett Bank plc (78825 G) to Banque de Paris (51144 BANPAR F) confirming that Mrs Gail Lovett will visit the Head Office of Banque de Paris in Rue de Rivoli, Paris, on 25.11.— at 10.00 a.m. to meet Mr Laurent Dubois.

Practice from the paper

Please send a telex message to the Bayview Hotel, Harbour Approach, Kowloon, Hong Kong, cancelling the two week stay of your Accounts Manager Mrs Rosemary Kee, which was due to start on August 1st, and instead reserving a room for her for one week from August 8th.

NB You do not need to give telex or answerback numbers in your answer, but simply the wording of the message.

Check your success

Is the wording brief? ☐

Is the wording entirely clear? ☐

Are all relevant details included? ☐

If you have used abbreviations, are these clearly understandable? ☐

9 International telegrams and telemessages

9.1 International telegrams

Understand how and why to send an international telegram.

An international telegram is a speedy and reliable way of communicating brief but urgent information through a reliable medium. In the UK this service is run by British Telecom.

First you need to dictate your message by telephone to the International Telegram department of British Telecom. You must provide the name and postal address of the person or company you are trying to contact.

The text of the telegram is then despatched electronically to a receiving office in the country concerned, which prints the message out, and delivers it by postal or courier service.

Advantages

- It enables speedy written communication over long distances.
- It can reach destinations on the basis of a postal address only. (This cannot be done by telex or facsimile transmission, both of which require a specialist machine at the receiving address.)

As telegrams are charged according to their number of words, international telegrams frequently use abbreviations to cut down the length and costs of a message. While the address of the recipient must be written in full to ensure prompt and correct delivery, the message itself can be easily abbreviated.

Example

The following instruction arrives on Winston Davies' desk:

Please send int'l telegram to Becky Deane of our associate company Hilmont Glass Ltd. Becky is on holiday with friends at Flat 5, 72 Via Erimi, Verona, Italy. Tell her to call at the Milan office of Hilmont Glass to collect the new designs for our new range of vases and table decorations from Signor Rivera. He expects her at 11.00 am on August 18th, as her flight leaves Milan that afternoon.
Thanks. Teresa Parkland. Head of Design.

Winston redesigns the message as an international telegram as follows:

34 English for business communications

BECKY DEANE, FLAT 5, 72 VIA ERIMI, VERONA, ITALY.

COLLECT NEW VASE/TABLE DESIGNS 19 AUGUST 11.30 MILAN
VIA GARIBALDI OFFICE FROM SIG. RIVERA. THANKS, PARKER.

All the relevant facts are presented, but wording is condensed to be as brief as possible.

Test your competence

Draft international telegrams for the following purposes.

1 You are Malcolm Lowry, Senior Manager at Pirelo Tyre Company. You need to contact your colleague Anita Patel who is staying at 15 Chatham Road, Kowloon Hong Kong, to advise her that a delivery of sample brochures will arrive for collection at Hong Kong airport on flight CP500 from London, due at 15.30 hours on March 3rd. Ask her to collect the package from the airline, and to take some identification to the airport. (25 words including address.)

2 While on a riding holiday in France, Marina Warner has broken an ankle. Send an international telegram from the Group Leader, Mrs Jill Horrocks, to Mrs Patricia Warner, 5 Hoskins Road, Ampton AO6 1BZ advising her of the accident, and explaining that Marina has had medical treatment and is comfortable but that her leg will be in plaster for three weeks. The telephone number of Hotel Bretagne, Quimper, France where you are staying is 54–44821.

9.2 Telemessages Understand how and why to send a telemessage

Telemessages are similar to international telegrams, but are available only within the UK. The wording of the message, and the name and full postal address of the recipient are dictated over the telephone to the Telemessage operator, who sends the message through the Telemessage network to the centre nearest to the recipient. The message is then printed out and delivered by the postal service to the addressee. Delivery is guaranteed on the day following the dictating of the message.

Telemessages are a speedy and useful way of contacting someone within the UK when there is no available telephone. Like international telegrams they are charged by the word, and so an abbreviated form of wording is usual.

Example

TO: JAMES OGREBOR, 124 ALGERNON RD, LONDON SE13 2DK. PLEASE CONTACT US URGENTLY ON 644 6678 REGARDING YOUR HOUSE MOVE. WE NEED YOU TO MAKE AN APPOINTMENT TO SIGN A MORTGAGE DOCUMENT IN OUR OFFICES. REGARDS, LEE AND BEAVIS, SOLICITORS.

Test your competence

Malik and Jackson are a small wine merchants in Bristol. Simon Malik needs to contact his partner Antonia Jackson urgently to seek her approval for some wines he wants to buy. He has reserved the wines – 480 bottles of French Burgundy (1974) at a bargain price of £5.30 per bottle. But cash must be paid by 18.00 hours on the following day. Antonia is on a walking holiday based at the Highland Lodge Hotel, Butle, near Pitlochry, Scotland.

Draft a brief telemessage for Simon Malik to send to Antonia.

Practice from the paper

You have discovered that an urgent box of supplies has not been posted. Send a telegram of not more than 15 words to Joseph Lokano, 151 Adelphi Street, Hong Kong, telling him that Box No 19462 will be despatched on the same day as the telegram. Apologise for the error.

Check your success

Did you include Joseph Lokano's address in full? ☐

Are all details included? ☐

Have you condensed the wording? ☐

10 Formal Invitations

Recognise the appropriate style to be used for invitations and ensure that all the relevant details are included.

Formal invitations are issued by individuals or organisations to mark a special occasion. They are generally issued on a single piece of card, advising the recipient of the invitation of the **date**, **time**, **location** and nature of the function. They almost always conclude with the initials RSVP, an abbreviation of the French phrase, 'Repondez, s'il vous plait', meaning 'Please Reply.'

Invitations are brief and essentially simple items of correspondence, and can be answered equally simply.

Example

```
            THE DIRECTORS OF ADSERVE LIMITED
            request the pleasure of the company of

                   MR AND MRS G J DUJOHN

        at an official reception to mark the opening of
              the new showroom, to be held at

              124 TRAFALGAR ROAD, LONDON SE10 6NY

             on Monday 16 September 19- at 6.30p.m.

                Cocktails and canapes will be served.

              RSVP to Fiona Ayling on 01 633 5922, or
            by writing to her at ADSERVE, 5 Victoria Way,
                          London SE7 9RJ.
```

An example of a written reply to this invitation would be

Formal invitations 37

```
                                    53 Lamming Gardens
                                    London SE8 0FR
                                    Tel:   693 5411


                                    6 September 19-


              Mr and Mrs G Dujohn

    acknowledge the receipt of your kind invitation to the Adserve
         reception on 16 September, and will be pleased to attend.
```

Alternatively, a simple business letter, with the subject heading 'ADSERVE RECEPTION' could be sent.

Test your competence

1 Design an invitation to the 50th anniversary celebration dinner and dance of Benting's department store. The celebration will be held on the evening of Saturday July 11th 19— in the restaurant at the store, High Street Ildale, Essex IL2JB, and will start at 7.30 pm.

2 Bellamy's car dealers, The Strand, Cromer, Norfolk NO5J2 wants to invite local businessmen to an exhibition and launch of a new Japanese car, the Dashazi Dart, on Tuesday 18th May at 12.30 pm, followed by a buffet lunch. As test drives in the car will be available on request, only soft drinks, tea and coffee will be served before and during the buffet.

Practice from the paper

Your employer, Miss J Wilkinson, of Messrs Wilkinson & Sons, has been invited to a Press Conference next Monday. She has asked you to reply on her behalf, in a formal way. The invitation came from Bain's Boutique Ltd, Bain's House, Broad Street, Folkestone, Kent, FK9 3OA. Miss Wilkinson will be going to the Conference.

Check your success

Have you set the acceptance out informally, either as a formal reply or as a letter?

Have you included all the necessary details?

Have you maintained formality in tone?

11 Letters of adjustment or apology

Understand the principles to be applied when writing letters of adjustment or apology and recognise their purpose.

Before reading this unit make sure you have read and fully understand units 4–6 on the basic principles of business letters.

A letter of adjustment is written when an organisation needs to amend an existing practice or state of affairs. It aims to achieve two objectives:
- to explain or clarify what has gone wrong, and why an adjustment is needed
- to define what the adjustment will be

Letters of adjustment can take several forms. A company may write a letter of adjustment after it has received a complaint (*see letters of complaint* later in this guide). In this case, the letter of adjustment will attempt to improve the relationship with the complainant, perhaps by offering a response to the complaint in the form of a refund or replacement.

Alternatively, a letter of adjustment may simply amend a business relationship, or explain a change in business procedure. An example is a letter written by a business organisation to explain a change in address or in company organisation to its customers. The following principles should be applied when writing letters of adjustment or apology:
- open by explaining why an adjustment to previous practice has been decided
- explain exactly which aspects of previous arrangements are to be changed
- explain the effect of the change upon the recipient of the letter
- try to maintain a good relationship with the recipient by expressing a suitable tone. This may be *conciliatory* if the letter is a response to a complaint or *reassuring*, if the adjustment is an unexpected change.

The need to fulfil these principles frequently results in letters that are arranged in the form of several paragraphs, even though a simple adjustment is the underlying reason for the letter.

Example

United Dairies Ltd
Farmfresh House
Progress Drive
Halvale
West Yorkshire HA3 4JS

Established 1912   Tel: 076 4998

WP/FH

Dear Customer

For over thirty years, we have sold and delivered milk to you, our valued customers, in pint glass bottles. Recently, however, the disadvantages of this form of packaging your milk have become clear to us. Glass is now a relatively expensive material, and it is also heavier than other suitable materials, so adding to our transportation and delivery costs. We also lose too much milk through breakages to glass, which results in higher costs for us to contain.

We have therefore decided that, as from June 1st 19-, all our milk will be packaged and delivered in cardboard cartons. This will include milk delivered to your doorstep.

This change will help us to avoid cost increases that we would otherwise have to pass on to you. It also means that our early morning deliveries of milk will be quicker, more efficient and quieter. Another advantage is that milk will be available in three sizes: the traditional pint size, a one-litre carton and a two-litre carton. Please let your milkman know which size of carton you would like.

At UNITED DAIRIES we are very pleased about the improved service this change will bring. We hope you like the new cartons, and of course, please remember that the milk inside them is just the same high quality product that we have given you for over seventy five years!

With best wishes

Wilfred Pickles.

Wilfred Pickles
Customer Relations Manager

You will see that the letter is sectioned into paragraphs, each paragraph fulfilling a separate function:

Paragraph 1: explains need for adjustment

Paragraph 2: defines and details adjustment

Paragraph 3: explains the advantages of the new arrangements

Paragraph 4: offers reassurance.

Test your competence

Write the following letters of adjustment.

1 Thornham Insurance Brokers Ltd of 55–58 The Rise, Wokingham SURREY GU6 4EJ are moving to occupy new offices at Suite 5, The Cornhill Centre, Guildford, Surrey GU1 7UT. The company will move on December 9th 19—, and will open for business on December 10th. The new telephone number will be Guildford 28434. The move will be accompanied by the introduction of a new computerised records system for all clients, which will cut the company's overhead costs by an estimated 15% and enable it to handle correspondence much more easily.

Produce a letter to be circulated to all the company's clients, signed by Mr Clive Thornham, the Chairman.

2 Write a letter from Capricorn Shipping Ltd, 55, The New Trading Estate, Mombasa, Kenya to Goonting Textiles Ltd, of 13–18 Penang Road, Kuala Lumpur, Malaysia. Explain that as from the first of next month warehouse fees for storage of their textiles will increase from a monthly rate of US$ 400 per container to US$ 430. The new rate will, however, include full insurance cover against fire and theft. Explain that invoices will be issued at the new rate as from the first of the following month.

Practice from the paper

Your employer, the owner of a bookshop, wishes to let his regular customers know that a sale will be held next month. He has asked you to draft a letter which he can send to all customers telling them of the sale. It will take place for one month and large discounts will be available. Draft the letter for Mr J Jones, Jones Bookshop Ltd, 9 The Alley, Nantwich, Cheshire, DT3 5BL. Do not give any name and address of the recipient, but simply begin with Dear . . . .

Check your success

Have you included the sender's address? ☐

Does the letter have all necessary aspects of layouts, including: ☐

    Reference ☐

    Subject heading ☐

    Salutation ☐

    Subscription? ☐

Is the letter sectioned into paragraphs which announce the sale? ☐

Does the letter give: ☐

    Details of dates, times and other details as appropriate? ☐

    Other encouragement to attend? ☐

12 Letters of complaint

Understand the principles to be applied when writing letters of complaint.

Letters of complaint are very common in business, particularly in those businesses which deal at first hand with the general public, which frequently receive and act on letters of complaint.

A letter of complaint is similar to a letter of adjustment, in that it is written with the aim of securing a change in the current situation or relationship between one business and another, or between a business and a customer. A letter of complaint is always caused by dissatisfaction on the part of the writer with the quality of goods or services that he has received. The following principles should be considered when writing letters of complaint:

1 The letter must express clearly and precisely the nature of the writer's dissatisfaction. A generalised expression of dissatisfaction is of little use, as it offers no guidance to the recipients, who may well be keen to remedy the complaint, if they receive sufficient information.

2 It should always provide relevant details regarding *date*, *time* and *place*. Often, dates and times of purchase of an article, or of the inadequate or unsatisfactory provision of a service, will be necessary.

3 While a letter of complaint should clearly express the writer's dissatisfaction (and may therefore, be direct and even forceful in tone) it should always remain courteous and controlled.

4 A letter of complaint should not only express a complaint, but should also request or suggest an adjustment. The writer should make clear to the recipient how, in the writer's view, the recipient should respond to the complaint. A letter of complaint should therefore be seen as a document which is starting a process of adjustment, in the expectation that the recipient will follow up and remedy the complaint.

Example

Yardle Ltd
Soap and Perfume Manufacturers
5–12 Advance Way, Tipton ESSEX CH4 6TY
Tel: (0236) 68528

```
The Manager
Hotel Constellation
Tipton ESSEX CH5
```

Dear Sir

CHRISTMAS DINNER AND DANCE

I write regarding this function, which was held as usual at your hotel on 23 December last year, and attended by 270 of our employees.

Unfortunately, there was widespread dissatisfaction with some aspects of the occasion, and I am sure you will want to know the details. The difficulties centred around three aspects of the evening, as follows:

1. Although a dining time of 8.30p.m. had been agreed, more than seventy of our guests did not receive any food until after 9.10p.m. This meant that they became very hungry, and also that food, when it did arrive, was frequently quite cold.

2. For dessert a choice of ice cream, fruit salad or cheese and biscuits was offered. As the occasion was two days before Christmas, and as it had been booked as a Christmas dinner, this was an extremely disappointing and unimaginative menu. The least we might have expected was a choice including traditional Christmas food such as Christmas pudding or mince pies.

3. We had specified that we required a dance band to play traditional dance music. The band, 'STOMPER JONES AND THE HEAVY BRIGADE', in fact played only modern rock music, to which it was difficult or impossible to dance.

It is fair to say that these three failings diminished the enjoyment of the evening for some, and ruined it for many. This is particularly disappointing, as we have used the Constellation for the past seven years.

The Christmas dinner/dance is one occasion when Yardle's entertains (and pays for) its employees. We are therefore writing to request you to **refund 20%** of our total payment of £6750.00 for the evening, a sum of £1350.00.

We are sure that, in the interests of goodwill and continued business relations between Yardle's and the Constellation, you will agree to make this refund. We look forward to hearing from you shortly.

Yours sincerely

N. Beasley

Nicole Beasley
Personnel Director

This a good letter of complaint because
- it specifies the exact nature of the complaint, with relevant details, dates and times
- it suggests a clear course of remedial action for the recipient
- it explains why remedial action is in the interests of the recipient
- the tone, while firm and clearly dissatisfied, remains controlled and courteous

Letters of complaint 43

Test your competence

Write the following letters of complaint:

1 You have just returned from a holiday in Spain organised by Vista Tours, 18 Berkeley Square, London W1A 3RG. Your holiday was booked to include all meals. On arrival at your hotel, you found that breakfast only was served throughout the two weeks of your stay. This was very inconvenient, as a member of your party was disabled, and had to be pushed by wheelchair to a local restaurant for all other meals. Write a letter of complaint, proposing remedial action. Invent details as necessary.

2 You are Buying Director of KIDSHOP, a nationwide chain of toy stores with Head Office at 67 Temple Drive, Bristol BR6 RT. You have ordered 5,000 model walking spacemen, a remote controlled toy powered by battery, from Zenith Toys Ltd, 18–34 Delaware Drive, Trenton, New Jersey, USA. The toys have been delivered, but on inspection you find that 1,200 of them have faulty electrical connections. A further 200 have been damaged beyond repair in transit. Write a letter of complaint to Mr Ed Sneadman, the Managing Director.

Practice from the paper

Write a letter from a firm of car manufacturers to a manufacturer of industrial paint, who has been asked to supply metallic paint for a new model of car. Your firm needs the paint urgently, and it is seven weeks overdue. State the situation in a suitable tone, and insist on delivery within one week. Explain that alternatively, you will cancel the order and use another paint manufacturer.

Check your success

Is your letter correctly laid out? ☐

Does it specify the exact nature of the complaint? ☐

Does it suggest a clear course of remedial action? ☐

Is the tone firm, while controlled and courteous? ☐

Are alternatives clearly explained? ☐

13 Letters of explanation

Understand the principles to be applied when writing letters of explanation.

A letter of explanation is a letter which conveys detailed explanatory information to its recipients in an official form.

Letters of explanation are among the most frequent items of business communication. This is because there are many occasions in all types of business where it is necessary to explain an issue in a **precise**, **detailed**, **permanent** and **official** way. These four requirements are best met by the letter, in which the following principles should be noted:

- an explanation must be made in terms that are clear. Letters of explanation are frequently written in order to clear up confusion or misunderstanding, and they are unsuccessful if they do not fully **clarify** an issue that may be complex or involved.
- explanations frequently need to be **detailed** so letters of explanation must accurately record all necessary details.
- **organisation** is usually important in a letter of explanation. A good explanatory letter clearly introduces the subject, and then systematically covers all aspects that need to be explained. This often involves careful sequencing of points and careful paragraphing (*see unit 5*).
- a good letter of explanation often gives the **reasons** for the situation it is explaining, and thereby preserves good relations with the recipient.

Example

The following is an example of a letter of explanation, written by a manufacturer of electrical goods to its retailers:

```
                    Morrison Electrical Limited
                 Mill Lane, Maidstone, Kent MA3 7TF

                      Telephone: (9473) 468572
                      Fax: (9473) 458621

To:    All Retailers
       Morrison Products

Dear Retailer

MORRISON ELECTRIC IRON, MODEL 385/S

The above model is one of our range of electrical steam irons for
domestic use.  We are writing to advise retailers of changes in the
model, which will be effective in models delivered from our factory
after 1 September 19-.  The changes are as follows:
```

1. The new model will need to be wired to a plug with a 5 amp. fuse, and not a 13 amp fuse as previously. This is due to our use of a new type of electrical element in the iron.

2. When filling the irons with water, it will no longer be necessary to use distilled water. All irons will function safely and effectively on ordinary tap water, and will require no special cleaning or de-scaling as a result. This is because of a new manufacturing process which eliminates scaling.

Please note that these points will be clearly covered in the 'Instructions for Use' brochure accompanying the irons, and also in a heavy advertising campaign we will be mounting during September.

Should you have any further queries on these changes, or indeed on any of our goods, please feel free to contact me on the above telephone number.

Yours sincerely

Denis Chan

Denis Chan
Technical Services Manager

This is a successful letter of explanation because
- it introduces the subject clearly at the start of the letter
- it is structured carefully into sections, to explain each change in detail
- it details the reasons behind each of the points explained.

Test your competence

1 You are the Customer Relations Manager of Modernmode Ltd, a chain of modern clothing shops with branches in major cities. For the past three years the company has run fashion evenings for all customers holding accounts with the store. These evenings have been very popular with customers, as they have been able to visit the store, have complimentary refreshments, see fashion displays and purchase in relaxed and uncrowded conditions.

However, the company has decided that these evenings are too expensive to continue, as it has to pay overtime rates to its fashion models, and to store assistants and security staff. The evenings have also achieved relatively disappointing sales.

Write a letter to be circulated to all Account Customers, from Modernmode Head Office at 52 Baker Street, London W1, explaining the need for the change, and assuring customers that other special benefits for account customers, including a 5% discount arrangement, will soon be established.

2 You are Personnel Officer in Murmay, a large industrial factory. The firm's canteen is to be closed for three weeks to permit a total refit of the kitchens and redecoration of the canteen area. Draft a letter to circulate to the workforce which explains the reasons for the closure, and the long term benefits which will follow. The canteen will close at 17.00 hours on October 15th, and re-open on November 3rd at 8.00 hours.

Practice from the paper

Write a letter from the Healthcover Insurance Company, 90 George Road, Dublin to all policyholders. Explain that Healthcover has been taken over by a larger international insurance group, ALLCO Insurance Inc of the USA. As a result of the takeover, the Dublin offices will be closed and all Irish policies will be administered from ALLCO offices in London. However, the nature of the insurance cover will remain the same. Write in a reassuring tone, and point out that the takeover will result in a reduction of costs, due to ALLCO's computer systems. Thank policyholders for their support of the Dublin office in the past.

Check your success

- Is the letter appropriately set out? ☐
- Does the letter begin by describing the change in brief, clear terms? ☐
- Does the letter go on to explain the reasons for the change? ☐
- Does the letter stress the advantages of the change to the recipient? ☐
- Is the letter reassuring in its tone? ☐

14 Sales and promotional letters

Understand the principles to be applied when writing sales and promotional letters.

Sales and promotional letters are written to advertise products or services, and to encourage the recipient to buy or use them. The following principles apply to such letters.
- sales and promotional letters always list the advantages of the product or service they describe. These advantages may be presented with particular reference to the circumstances or needs of the recipient of the letter.
- a good sales letter presents these advantages in a convincing, but not aggressive, manner, and therefore is written in a tone that is positive, but controlled.
- a sales letter generally closes by inviting the recipient to respond. This invitation may be in the form of a concluding paragraph inviting the recipient to telephone for a trial or sample, or a tear off slip (sometimes called a coupon) attached to the foot of the letter, which encourages the recipient to place an order or seek further details.
- such letters often include details of pricing.

Example Look at this promotional letter, sent out by an insurance company.

Safeguard Insurance Limited
Safeguard House, County Drive, Poole, Dorset BH5 34F

Tel: (0546) 286429
Fax: (0546) 512319

```
Dear Customer

Would you like to save £100.00 per year on Motor Insurance?

At Safeguard, we can offer you low cost Motor Insurance, which
is likely to be as much as £100 per year below your current premium
cost.  We can make these savings as we ONLY offer insurance to
drivers like yourself:  people over the age of 30, who are
responsible, careful and dependable.

Our company has existed for fifty years, and all our policies are
guaranteed by Lloyds of London:  so you know your insurer is
dependable, and will meet your claim in the unlikely event that you
will need us.
```

48   English for business communications

Why not telephone us for a quotation? Put through a reverse charge call to us today, and join the thousands of other adults who are saving large sums of money, staying safe with SAFEGUARD.
We really would welcome a call from you.

Yours sincerely

James Brenton

James BRENTON
New Business Department

This sales letter is reasonably brief, and makes its point clearly. It identifies the advantage which it is trying to promote (economy), and it invites the recipient to reply. Although it is written positively, it is not excessive in tone.

Test your competence

1 Your company has recently designed a lawn mower for use in public parks and sports grounds. Called 'The Trekker', the mower is fitted with an efficient diesel engine that makes it economic to run and reliable. It needs servicing only two-yearly and the cutting blades on the mower can be removed for sharpening quickly and easily. The mower's other feature is that it collects loose twigs and leaves, and sifts them into a refuse basket attachment.

Write a sales letter promoting 'The Trekker', for circulation to sports clubs and the Parks Departments of local authorities. Your company is Quality Mowers Ltd of The Rise, Yeovil, Somerset TA3 7RN. The normal price of the mower is £2200, but for orders placed within a month, a 10% discount is available, with a 20% discount if more than one mower is ordered. Trials can be arranged.

2 You are Librarian at Progress College, where there are 2000 full time students. To create more shelf space, you are selling 8000 of the library's old stock. The books are on display in the library basement, which is open every day from 10.00 until 16.00. Most of the books are still recommended reading for current college courses, although 10% are light fictional reading. Prices will be very low to enable the stock to be sold quickly.

Write a sales letter to be sent to every student.

Practice from the paper

On 4 February Far & Wide Travel, a firm which arranges package holidays, was informed that the Seaside Hotel at Montego Bay, which was to be used during the forthcoming season, had been badly damaged by a hurricane and would not therefore be available to accommodate their clients.

As secretary to the Sales Manager, prepare a circular letter to be sent to clients who have reserved holidays at this hotel. Explain that a limited number of vacancies are available at other hotels; holiday price unchanged;

same amenities and standards, etc; some hotels away from beach; 5 kms from Montego Bay; have swimming pools etc; free transport provided from hotel to coast during holiday; 20% discount given if booked immediately; money refunded; deposits returned.

Check your success

Is the letter appropriately set out? ☐

Does the letter apologise for the change? ☐

Does the letter stress that the change is unavoidable? ☐

Does the letter clearly list the compensatory offers that the company is making? ☐

Does the letter clearly explain the option of cancellation that is open to customers? ☐

Does the letter finish with a positive wish to keep the recipient as a customer? ☐

15 Elementary examination questions

The following **elementary** examination paper has been worked through with solutions provided, giving helpful pointers for candidates.

It is suggested that you use the paper with model answers as follows:
1 Attempt an individual question.
2 Compare your answer with the model answer.

Please note that these are model answers only and in no way do they carry the authority of the Examining Board.

ENGLISH FOR BUSINESS COMMUNICATIONS
ELEMENTARY

No 130 EBC

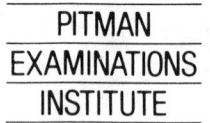

This paper must be returned with the candidate's work, otherwise the entry will be void and no result will be issued.

PITMAN EXAMINATIONS INSTITUTE

CANDIDATE'S NAME ....
(Block letters please)

CENTRE NO .... DATE ....

Time allowed: <u>2 hours</u>.

Answer <u>ALL</u> the questions in PART I.

In PART II answer Question 1 and <u>THREE</u> others.

All your answers must be written in <u>ink</u>.

Ensure that your name is written clearly at the top of each of your answer sheets.

Please note that marks may be deducted for untidy or illegible work.

<u>PART I</u>   (20 marks)

Using the twenty words below fill in the spaces in the following passage. <u>Each word can only be used once</u>.

outdated	computer	retrieve	security
burnt	tricked	information	documents
confidential	authorised	convenient	telephone
senior	reports	privately	lock
instructions	filing	minutes	shredding

Much of the .... dealt with in an office is of a ....

nature and it is very important that it should remain so. Sometimes when a

confidential .... call is received other people are within hearing.

You could ask the caller to ring back at a more .... time or you could

ask them to hold while you move to a more .... situated extension.

Confidential .... must be kept under .... and key at all

times in their own private .... system. Usually only ....

staff will have access to them. Care should be taken not to leave ....,

(Continued)

© Sir Isaac Pitman Ltd. 1988   F/HH/DMP letters, company accounts and .... of meetings on desk tops where they could be read by anyone who is passing. When confidential documents have become .... they should always be .... or put through a .... machine. Obviously a .... member of staff should give the .... for this to be done. In the modern office one source of confidential information is that which is kept on .... Such data can be tapped and read by anyone who has the knowledge of how to .... it. Confidential computers should be kept in a separate protected .... room as a great deal of damage can be done if the information stored falls into the wrong hands. Anyone who is in possession of confidential information should take care that they are not .... into divulging all or part of it.

PART II

Answer Question 1 and THREE others. It is advisable to start each answer on a clean sheet.

1. Write a letter from the Purchasing Manager, Mr James Jones, of Quick Assembly Kitchens, 92 London Road, Berkhamstead, BS4 6TU to the Sales Manager of Browns Timber Ltd, Maldon Road, Stevenage, complaining about the quality of the last delivery of teak finish wood they have received from the firm. In the past the quality of goods has always been very good but if the quality is not up to the required standard the firm will have to look elsewhere for a supplier.

    (23 marks)

2. The Garage Manager, Mr J Ryan has discovered that many of the garage mechanics are abusing the 5 minute rule which allows them time to wash up at the end of the morning and afternoon sessions. They are stopping work at least 10 minutes early. Write a memorandum from him to all the garage staff reminding them of the rule and informing them that the 5 minute allowance will be stopped if the abuse does not cease at once. A firm tone is needed.

    (19 marks)

(Continued)

3   You have recently started work in a large Insurance Company. Write a letter to your former Business Studies teacher describing your job and telling her how you are getting on in the world of work.

(19 marks)

4   You work for the Ace School of Driving, 20 Trinity Road, Wethersfield, Suffolk, WJ2 5TJ. Send a telex to the Sales Manager, Mr Ager of Fastprint Processing, Abbey House, Bury-St-Edmunds, BE7 4BS using the following notes.

Order No 761JDX - urgently needed for new publicity campaign in area - expected delivery a week ago. Is there any reason for this delay - an immediate reply is requested.

(19 marks)

5   Your employer Mr B Turnbridge of Turnbridge and Scott, Architects, Pinacle House, High Road, Watford, WE6 9PL, wishes to have information about a new photocopier he has seen advertised in Business World. Write a letter to the Manager, Excell Copiers, Newbridge Office Block, Luton, LU5 7RF, explaining where Mr Turnbridge saw the advertisement and asking for details of the XR66 machine. It is most important that the copier they buy is able to reduce and enlarge easily. A demonstration would be appreciated if this is possible.

(19 marks)

6   You are the Personnel Officer of your firm. Prepare a draft for the invitation that will be sent to all staff inviting them to the Annual Dinner and Dance to be held on 4 July next.

(19 marks)

Worked solutions   **1.1** information – confidential – telephone – convenient – privately – documents – lock – filing – authorised – reports – minutes – outdated – burnt – shredding – senior – instruction – computer – retrieve – security – tricked.

2.1

Quick Assembly Kitchens
92 London Road
Berkhamstead
BS4 6TU

7 April 19-

The Sales Manager
Browns Timber Limited
Maldon Road
Stevenage

Our ref: JJ/RLE

Dear Sir

TEAK FINISH WOOD

We have used your company as a supplier of teak wood for several years, and the quality of the wood has always been very good.

However, we took delivery of some wood from you on 3 April this year which was of poor quality. Many of the wood sections were chipped or scratched, and therefore impossible to use in making high quality kitchen finishes.

I do hope that this was an exceptional occasion, and that your supplies to us in future will always be of acceptable quality. If we do receive any further sub-standard supplies from you, we will be obliged to find another supplier who can provide us with goods which meet our own high standards.

Yours faithfully

James Jones

James Jones
Purchasing Manager

Elementary examination questions

2.2

MEMORANDUM

To: All staff   Date: 11/11/-

From: Garage Manager

Subject: WASHING UP TIME

It has become clear that many members of staff are abusing the privilege of washing up time.

Washing up time is strictly limited to five minutes at the end of the morning and afternoon sessions. Many staff are stopping work at least ten minutes early. All staff should be able to complete washing up within the five minutes which the company allocates for this purpose.

It should be remembered that washing up time is a privilege, and that staff are paid during this time. If it is not possible to keep the washing up period within its five minute limit, the company will consider the complete withdrawal of this privilege.

J Ryan

2.3

65 Redstone Terrace
Larching
Bedfordshire   LLT 3RY

Mrs L Ferrera
Business Studies Department
Larching School
Bedfordshire   LLT 8HD

Dear Mrs Ferrera

I have now been working in the Claims Department of the Orion Insurance Company for three months and I thought you would like to know how I am getting on.

The job is much more interesting than I had expected. When I joined, I expected to be doing routine filing and typing but, in fact, there is much more to the job than that. I have to inspect claim forms which come in from people who have had accidents or illnesses. Firstly, I have to check that they have filled in the forms correctly. If not, I have to compose a careful letter to them explaining what they have omitted.

Once a complete form has come in, I have to check that the person claiming is still covered by one of our policies, and then comes the most interesting part of the job. I have to read through the form and decide whether the

56 English for business communications

claim for damage, medical expenses or other costs loooks to be accurate. If it seems wrong, or it is not supported by receipts or repair estimates, I send it to my superior for checking.

So you can see that there is a lot of care and thought involved, and I am very grateful for all the training I had in these areas at school.

After another three months I will have the chance to train to be a Senior Claims Clerk. This will involve a four-day course at Head Office in London, and a pay rise if I am successful!

So I am really very happy with the way that everything has worked out for me and I would like you to pass on my thanks to all the staff at Larching. I do hope to see you again in the future.

Yours sincerely

Mercy Uzumu

Mercy Uzumu

2.4

```
        TELEX        21.9.-

        TO: MR AGER, SALES, FASTPRINT PROCESSING.    TELEX 2349

        WE URGENTLY NEED ORDER 761 JDX FOR OUR NEW LOCAL PUBLICITY
CAMPAIGN.  DELIVERY WAS DUE 13.9.  WHY IS THERE NO DELIVERY?  PLEASE
RESPOND URGENTLY.

        R JONES. ACE SCHOOL OF DRIVING.  TELEX 6815
```

2.5

```
                    TURNBRIDGE AND SCOTT (ARCHITECTS)
                  PINNACLE HOUSE  HIGH ROAD  WATFORD  WE6 9PL
                              TEL: 4876 85734
```

The Manager
Excell Copiers
Newbridge Office Block
Luton   LU5 7RF

Our ref: PHJ/GK

Dear Sir

<u>XR66 PHOTOCOPIER</u>

I am writing on behalf of my employer Mr B Turnbridge, who is most interested in the XR66 copier. He saw the machine advertised in a recent edition of <u>Business World</u>.

We have a particular need for a machine that can reduce and enlarge easily, and it is likely that the XR66 would meet our requirements. We would therefore be very glad if you could send us full details of this machine, including costings.

We would also be very grateful for a demonstration of the machine, either at our offices or at your own showrooms. Please let us know if this can be arranged.

Yours sincerely

P. Harrison

Philip Harrison
Office Manager

2.6

THE DIRECTORS OF BROWNLAND LIMITED

request the pleasure of the company of

....

at the Brownland Annual Dinner and Dance to be held
at the Lincoln Rooms, Overland Road, Cheston
on 4 July 19–. from 8.00pm onwards.

———

Dress informal   RSVP Ms A Rowle, Personnel Dept

———

Part 2 Intermediate

Syllabus

English for Business Communications Intermediate

(Time allowed – 2½ hours)

At this stage candidates will be required to answer 2 compulsory questions, one a letter and one a report, and a further 3 from a choice of 5.

Candidates will be required to:

(a) Compose letters from brief notes dealing with general business matters, such as letters of complaint, enquiry, acceptances, sales letters, travel arrangements.
(b) Write personal letters for business employers, including letters of introduction and recommendation; letters of welcome, congratulations and seasonal greeting; formal replies to invitations.
(c) Compose memoranda.
(d) Write international telegrams, telex or other messages with confirmatory letters; telephone messages, advertisements.
(e) Write draft reports from information given.

Candidates should have the ability to read and analyse correspondence received by a company and assess the type of reply needed.

Checklist – Intermediate

	Unaided	Date	Aided	Date
16 Writing a letter from notes: organising and sectioning Write a business letter from notes making effective use of sectioning when organising the body of the letter.				
17 Style and tone Make effective use of style and tone in a business letter and use each of these appropriately.				
18 Writing reports Understand the purpose of reports and recognise their common features.				
19 Writing a memorandum from notes Recognise the purpose of the memorandum and write a memo based on notes you have been given.				
20 The international telegram (or telex) with a letter of confirmation Recognise the purpose of sending an international telegram or telex and understand the need for a letter of confirmation.				
21 Advertisements Understand how to write the text for an advertisement, with an appropriate balance between information and persuasion.				
22 Testimonials Understand the purpose of testimonials and the style of writing that should be adopted.				
23 Types of personal letter Write personal letters using the appropriate style and tone for each type.				

Instructions for Part 2

The Pitman Examinations Institute examination in English for Business Communication at Intermediate level shares many topics with the Elementary examination. Both examinations will test your ability to compose items of written correspondence such as letters, memoranda, reports and invitations, and to show a knowledge of correct layout. A sound grasp of the topics in the Elementary examination is ideal preparation for the Intermediate stage. Similarly, before embarking on this section of the Examination Guide, you should prepare by reading carefully through the section on the Elementary examination.

However, there are important differences in the Intermediate examination, which is naturally more demanding than the Elementary level. Examination questions at Intermediate level will *supply you with less information* than at Elementary level, and so you will need to develop and use **suitable material** of your own in written correspondence. (By contrast, the Elementary examination provides the candidate with almost *all* the information needed for a full answer.)

The ability to study an examination question and understand its problems and issues, and the ability to write original material based on this understanding, is a vital skill at Intermediate level.

At Intermediate level, there are *two* compulsory questions: a letter and a report. After these you will be required to choose three further questions from the five remaining on the paper.

Examiners at Intermediate level are concerned with your ability to compose written answers which are **effective** in dealing with the issue or issues underlying the question, and which are **appropriate** in their content, style and organisation.

Topics in the intermediate examination

The examination contains the following topics, which are covered in depth in this section.
- a compulsory **business letter**, written from brief notes in the question.
- a compulsory **report**, based on information given in the question.
- a **memorandum**, written from brief notes in the question.
- an **international telegram** plus a **letter of confirmation** OR a **telephone message** OR an **advertisement**
- **a personal letter** OR a **reply to an invitation**
- **a business letter** (on a *less involved* topic than the compulsory first question).
- a **report** (*briefer* than the compulsory report.)

62 English for business communications

16 Writing a letter from notes: organising and sectioning

Write a business letter from notes making effective use of sectioning when organising the body of the letter.

Writing a letter for the Intermediate examination will follow the same general principles as explained in units 3 and 4, but the exercise will be more lengthy and demanding, and examiners will look for aptitude in the areas of layout, content and style.

Layout should follow the basic principles of letter presentation outlined earlier. However, particular care needs to be taken with paragraphing and with organising the body of the letter. The notes that form part of the question will most likely need to be organised into several different sections in the body of the letter.

Candidates will therefore need to organise the body of the letter into distinct paragraph units, to reflect the separate issues within the question notes.

Example

The following question from a past examination paper provides a useful example.

Buildwell Brothers Ltd is a firm of wholesalers in Oldham supplying building materials and fittings to the building trade and to retailers. They have recently decided to move to new premises and to reorganise their business.

All customers are to receive a personalised letter from the Managing Director explaining the reorganisation and assuring them that this will result in better service than has been possible from the old premises.

Using the information given below write the letter to Black & White Ltd, 20/24 Abbey Road, Manchester, M26 3LB.

Administrative Headquarters in new premises at Buildwell House, Bridge Street, Oldham – phone 061–336–8866 – all accounts kept here.

Sales divided into four regions – Northern: Manager – Mr J Smith – phone 061–433–7700; Eastern: Manager – Mr D Piper – 024–572 3384; Southern: Manager – Mr W Brown – 045–950 9876; Western: Manager – Mr R Jones 053–215 0151.

Orders delivered; credit terms available – cash in 28 days – discount; Cash and Carry system to be introduced – customers collecting goods and paying cash allowed 1% cash discount – Trade Card necessary – apply to HQ if required.

These notes present a large volume of information. Unless it is organised into sections by competent paragraphing, the result will be an unwieldy and inefficient letter, which is difficult to read. However, the notes in this example could usefully be organised into the following sections:

1 details of address and location of accounts
2 organisation and details of sales department
3 systems for delivery, payment and discounts

The sectioning of the letter makes it easier to read and follow, more attractive on the page, and more memorable.

It is therefore crucial to study the question notes, and to plan the organisation and sectioning of the body of your letter in a way that reflects the subject matter, and which makes the subject matter easier for the reader.

Test your competence

The Board of Directors of Comfort Hotels Ltd have agreed to consult the managers of their 37 hotels in major world cities with a view to expanding facilities. Draft a letter for the Chief Executive to circulate to all hotel managers, outlining the proposed range of improvements for the chain of hotels, and asking for comments, including a view of the likely impact of the changes on the atmosphere of the hotels. Use the information outlined in the following notes:

> Agreed to expand facilities for business users – provide hourly rental of office services – computer and word processing, telex/fax transmission, conference and theatre rooms with facilities for video and overhead projectors. Health and exercise facilities to be expanded to benefit from current fitness boom. Each hotel to add weights room and sauna, bigger branches to have indoor heated pool where space permits. Need for better training of reception staff in all branches – wider range of reception skills should include knowledge of how to book theatre tickets, hire cars, fix day excursions and onward (international) travel for clients.

Practice from the paper

The Personnel Officer of Design & Production Ltd, Olympia Works, Cirencester, CR2 3BW, has received a letter from the Careers Adviser, Ash Tree Upper School, Ash Lane, Gloucester, GL1 2JQ, requesting assistance in arranging periods of work experience for 6th Form students following a course in Business Studies.

As Secretary to the Personnel Officer, you have been asked to draft the letter which he will send in reply to this request. Using the notes given below, draft the letter.

> Regret not possible at present; management recognises importance of work experience; Managing Director investigating suggestions put forward by Personnel Department; if scheme can be worked out, implemented as soon as possible; list of schools and colleges wishing to be included being compiled – Ash Tree Upper to be included; unlikely everybody can be accommodated this year.

Check your success

Is the letter correctly set out? ☐

Does one paragraph express regret and make clear that assistance is not possible? ☐

Does another paragraph explain the positive steps that are being taken? ☐

Is the tone of the letter positive, and likely to sustain a future relationship? ☐

17 Style and tone

Make effective use of style and tone in a business letter and use each of these appropriately.

A letter at Intermediate level is likely to carry a wide range of information, and may require the choice of a particular tone or style (*see* unit 6). For example, a letter of complaint may need to sound firm but courteous, and a letter of apology must sound sincere. The ability to control tone in the language of a letter is very important, especially as the tone may change within the letter itself.

Example

>   Nuke Shoes Ltd
>   Olympic House
>   Progress Parade
>   Livingston EH54 1TL
>
>   Tel: 051 842837
>
> Mr J Kendle
> 57 Chalsey Drive
> Coventry CO3 5TT
>   7 April 19-
>
> Our ref: PJ/HKD/7.4.-.
>
> Dear Mr Kendle
>
> Thank you for returning your pair of NUKE ADVANCE sports shoes to us for examination. We were sorry to hear that you were dissatisfied with the shoes, and in particular that you felt they had worn out too quickly.
>
> It is very unusual for us to receive complaints about our shoes, in fact we have had only seven pairs returned to us out of the eighty thousand pairs we have sold since the range was introduced three years ago. We note from the receipt you enclosed with the shoes that they were in fact purchased more than two years ago, in November 19-. Unfortunately, we are unable to replace shoes that are more than three months old, and I therefore cannot meet your request for a replacement pair of shoes.
>
> However, I am pleased to enclose a discount voucher to the value of £4.00, which can be used in the purchase of any item of NUKE footwear. We do hope that you will continue to use our products.
>
> Yours sincerely
>
> *Phyllis Jandu*
>
> PHYLLIS JANDU
> CUSTOMER SERVICES MANAGER

In this letter, the tone varies substantially from paragraph to paragraph, as follows:
- Paragraph 1: politely concerned
- Paragraph 2: assertive
- Paragraph 3: conciliatory

Control and variety of tone are vital to the effectiveness of this type of letter. If the tone is well managed, even a difficult and negative message, like the example shown above, can be expressed successfully.

Test your competence

You are Customer Accounts Manager for Trust Finance Ltd at 64 Market Street, Yeovil, Somerset TA12 5PU. A long-standing customer, Mr Peter Richards of The Old Mill, Barling, Somerset has failed to pay two successive monthly instalments, each of £85.60, on a loan he has taken from your company.

Write a letter to Mr Richards in which you point out the missed instalments and ask for immediate repayment. Present the request as courteously and diplomatically as possible, and attempt to close the letter with a positive statement that will maintain his goodwill and his custom.

Practice from the paper

A sales representative, Mr Jenson, from Kelmex Stationery Supplies Ltd, Maybury House, City Road, Upchester UP8 MN0, has been calling very frequently on the Purchasing Officer of your company, Brand Services Ltd, 96 Lemon Street, Milton, Beds, LU3 1BJ. Mr Jenson has been very persistent in his efforts to obtain an order for his goods, and his visits are becoming annoying.

Compose the letter which the Purchasing Officer will send to the Sales Manager of Kelmex Stationery Ltd, asking him to deal with this problem.

Check your success

Is the letter correctly set out?	☐
Does the opening paragraph explain the background facts of Mr Jenson's frequent visits?	☐
Does a different paragraph explain clearly that his visits are not welcomed?	☐
Does the letter clearly request that no further visits are made, unless by invitation?	☐
Does the tone remain courteous throughout?	☐

18 Writing reports

Understand the purpose of reports and recognise their common features.

A report is a business document written on a specified topic for a given audience. It may be brief enough to require only a single sheet of paper (such as an accident report completed for the Claims Department of an insurance company) or it may run to several hundred pages. All reports, however, share the following common features:

- a report opens with a section headed **terms of reference** – a brief explanation of what the report is about, and who is the intended audience.
- reports are organised in separate **sections** which are frequently introduced by section headings and numbered points or paragraphs.
- the **language** of reports is generally formal and official, without the variation in tone that is sometimes found within letters.
- some reports may conclude with a section headed **conclusions** and sometimes with a further paragraph making **recommendations** based on these. Other reports may be for information only, and will not feature these concluding sections.

In general, reports will have the following form:
1 Date and name or initials of writer
2 Terms of reference
3 Findings
4 Conclusion
5 Recommendations

Example

The following is a brief report written by a supermarket manager:

TESBURY PLC: NEWTOWN BRANCH

8.9.19-   DBJ/JMO

TERMS OF REFERENCE

To report to Area Manager (Mrs Juliet McDougall) on sales of biscuits in the period July-September 19-.

FINDINGS

1. The store took delivery of 1200 packs of Peanut Finger biscuits in June, which were prominently displayed throughout the sale period, accompanied by point of sale advertising signs. Although biscuit sales overall have risen by 12% in this period, the Peanut fingers sold only 370 boxes, well below our expectations. We are left with 830 boxes of out of date biscuits which we cannot sell.

```
2.  The 12% increase is largely explained by high sales over the
summer of traditionally popular biscuits (Digestive, Rich Tea, Lemon
Puff, etc.)

3.  One new line of biscuits which did sell reasonably well was the
Cherry Cracker, a new cherry flavoured sweet biscuit.  We took
delivery of 1200 packs and have sold 1085 packs at the same shelf
price (59p) as the Orange and Peanut fingers.

CONCLUSIONS

i    Our strong biscuit sales over the summer were based on
established and traditional types of biscuits.

ii   Of the two new brands, the Cherry Cracker has been far more
popular than the Peanut Finger.

            D. Juno
DEIRDRE JUNO, Manager, Newtown Branch.
```

Although this is a simple and brief report, the advantages of report form are clear.

Section headings — These are easy to read and follow and give the page a clear and attractive appearance. Although several different points of information are conveyed, the section headings allow the reader to grasp the points individually, and consider each point separately if necessary.

Numbered points — Like the section headings, the numbering of points allows a reader to distinguish one section of the report from another. Numbering can also enable a writer to show the reader the range and complexity of an issue. (In this report, the fact that the three separate headings are numbered shows the reader that the issue of biscuit sales is a complex and involved one.)

Formal tone — The tone is even and factual. It communicates in a clear and unemotional manner. It does not waste words, or allow feelings to cloud the issues.

Test your competence

1 Add a section headed 'Recommendations' to form section four of Deirdre Juno's report.

2 You are Junior Librarian at The University of Technology, at Leedvale in the UK. Using the notes below, write a letter to the Chief Librarian on the topic of library furniture. Include a section on recommendations at the end of the report.

Ground Floor: Periodicals Room seats only 20 – often there are as many as 10 students sitting on the floor. Armchairs in foyer area very comfortable – often contain students sleeping for 1–3 hours at a time.

First floor: Lighting in Geography section needs attention – four tubes out of twelve not working – students cannot easily read details on maps.

Basement: Much litter around photocopier and coffee machine, where

Writing reports 69

wastepaper bins are always full to bursting point. There is no carpet in the Biology section, so footsteps there often make a lot of noise and cause distraction to students.

Practice from the paper

Using the notes below write a report to the Export Sales Manager, outlining the ways in which the installation of telex could help to overcome the problems in his Department:

Telex messages typed – carbon copy kept for filing – confirmation unnecessary;

no difficulties hearing as with some telephone calls;

increasing number of firms now using telex machine – can be left unattended, but switched on to receive messages 24 hours; messages can be sent at any time, often by direct dialling;

present typists could be trained to operate machine;

costs of installation and annual rental probably less than wages of any additional staff; cost of calls probably offset by increased efficiency and additional business; suggest detailed investigation.

Check your success

Does the report open with Terms of Reference ☐

Is the report organised into numbered sections? ☐

Is the date included? ☐

Are the initials or signature of the writer included? ☐

Is the tone formal? ☐

19 Writing a memorandum

Recognise the purpose of the memorandum and write a memo based on notes you have been given.

The basics of preparing and writing a memorandum are covered in unit 7. In the Intermediate examination, the exercise involves writing a memorandum based on notes included in the question.

Remember that a memorandum is a purely internal document, used to convey information from one part of an organisation to another. It should be headed with **to** and **from** entries, should be **dated**, and should carry both a **reference** and a **subject heading**, as in this example.

```
                         MEMORANDUM

        FROM:   Thomas Mann                DATE:  15.12.19-
        TO:     All Departmental Managers  REF:   TM/JP
                    CHRISTMAS CLOSURE.

Please advise all staff that the factory and offices will
close at 13.00 hours on Monday 23 December and reopen at
8.00am on Thursday 2 January 19-.  It is important that
the site is cleared and locked by 14.00 on the 23rd.

                     TM
```

As a memorandum is an internal document, and does not involve public or customer relations, it is usually direct and factual in content, and neutral in tone.

Nevertheless, in some circumstances, control of tone may be necessary, especially when the memorandum is aimed at changing the habits and behaviour of staff.

Test your competence

Study the tone and organisation of the following memo:

MEMORANDUM

REF MC/ TJS

FROM: Michael Charlton, Managing Director.
TO: All Staff
DATE: 18 October 19-

SAFETY PROCEDURES.

I am sorry to tell you that two members of staff have suffered accidents in recent weeks. Teresa Sell, from our Stores Department, strained her back trying to lift a box of steel fittings without assistance. Also, last Thursday, Narendra Patel in the Despatch Department broke a toe in a fork lift truck accident.

These accidents are costly both to the company and to the individuals concerned. Please do make absolutely sure that you know all the safety procedures in your area of work.
We must improve the sloppy attitude to safety in the company. We cannot afford to lose more people on sick leave.   MC

This memo begins well, with the Managing Director sounding concerned, and illustrating the importance of safety in the workplace.

At the end of the memo, the tone lapses to one of criticism, and to the unfortunate closing comments, which suggests that the Managing Director is more concerned with time lost through sickness than with the safety and welfare of his staff. A memorandum that begins well loses its effectiveness through clumsily handled tone.

Rewrite Michael Charlton's memorandum, using a more careful tone to make all the necessary points, without sounding either too critical of the workforce, or unconcerned about their safety.

The memorandum written from notes in the examination may involve some care with tone.

Practice from the paper

Stationery is being wasted because all members of staff can make a verbal request at the Central Stores for any items required.

The Office Manager is seeking to improve matters by introducing a system for the regular ordering and supply of stationery, to come into operation on the first of next month. A Requisition Form must be signed by departmental supervisors, handed in to Central Stores before 1500 hrs for collection next day after 0930 hrs. For large orders advance notification is necessary, as is staff cooperation.

Compose the memorandum to be sent to all departmental supervisors, explaining the change of arrangements and setting out details of the scheme.

Check your success

- Is the memorandum correctly set out? ☐
- Is the style brief and to the point? ☐
- Does the memo open by describing the problem, and then go on to explain the new system? ☐
- Is the tone polite and controlled? ☐
- Does the tone avoid the possibility of offending the staff? ☐

20 The international telegram (or telex) with a letter of confirmation

Recognise the purpose of sending an international telegram or telex and understand the need for a letter of confirmation.

International telegrams and telexes are explained in detail in units 8 and 9. They provide a speedy, reliable means of conveying a brief written message to an international destination.

As they have to be extremely brief in order to contain costs, international telegrams (and, to a lesser extent, telexes) are often followed up by a letter of confirmation — a letter which confirms and explains in detail the points made speedily and economically by telegram. The letter of confirmation is a useful supplement to the telegram, and can fulfil the following purposes.
- provide a full level of detail to support the instructions in the telegram/telex at far lower cost
- communicate with more courteous and effective tone than a telegram or telex. The letter of confirmation is therefore likely to be more ambassadorial than the telegram, and hence a more effective means of maintaining relations between the sender and the recipient.

Example

Study the following examples of international telegrams and a confirming letter.

```
90-01-18  09:48
Msg 290 Title: AW2

R DAWSON.  HOTEL SUNRISE.  BANDAR BERI BAGAWAN, BRUNEI.
                                            28 APRIL 1991

PLEASE CANCEL AUSTRALIA VISIT 14-16 MAY.  RETURN LONDON FOR
EMERGENCY DIRECTORS' MEETING 8 MAY.  LETTER FOLLOWS.  REGARDS.
```

This international telegram or telex conveys the main point — the need for Mr Dawson to cancel the Australian phase of his business trip and return to London early. Now examine the follow-up letter of confirmation.

PJ and Partners Ltd
65 Queen Street
London EC2 3VT

```
Mr Raymond Dawson (Guest)
Hotel Sunrise
Bandar Seri Bagawan BRUNEI              23 April 19-

Dear Ray

I write following my telegram of today.

I am extremely sorry to have to ask you to return to London,
when I know how much you were looking forward to your marketing
trip to Australia.

The emergency is, I'm afraid, a tragic one.  Yesterday afternoon
both our Chairman, Peter Jameson, and the Managing Director,
Graham Gower, were killed in a car accident on the M6 motorway.
I know how this news will affect you, especially in view of the
close friendship you had with Graham.  I also know that you will
want to be at the funeral of both our colleagues, which will
be in London on 7 May.

The emergency Board of Directors meeting is being held to consider
how best to proceed in this situation.

I am sorry to have to give you this news, but I do look forward
to seeing you and working with you on your return to London.

Condolences and sincere regards.

          Mike

Michael Perry   Finance Director
```

This letter supports the telegram in two ways. First, it explains the background and details which necessitated the telegram.

Second, it can achieve a tone which would not be possible in the abbreviated telegram form.

Test your competence

Draft a telegram and a follow up letter in response to each of the following situations:

1 The New York office of your firm is Simons Brothers Incorporated, 526 Broadway Plaza, Broadway, NY 10012, USA. They are awaiting a contract from your office, which was due for despatch by international courier. After some confusion in your despatch department, the unsigned copy of the contract was sent, and the original signed copy was filed mistakenly in your office. Send a telegram explaining that the signed copy will arrive with a courier on board Pan American Airways flight no. PA 120 from London, arriving in New York at 16.50 hours the following day. Write a letter of confirmation and apology to Peter Simons, the senior partner in New York.

2 After returning from a business conference in Barbados, Mr Kenneth Greaves finds that he has brought home the briefcase of another delegate, M Francois Desfours of Pecartin et Cie, 15 Rue de Rivoli, Rennes, France.

Send a telegram to M Desfours explaining the mistake and advising him that his case is being returned to him by express courier. As your firm does a lot of business with Pecartin, you must preserve a good relationship with M Desfours. Write a follow up letter of apology and conciliation for the signature of Mr Greaves.

Practice from the paper

As a representative for Charles Hiller & Company Limited of Rolgate, Kent, RO1 3JK, you had promised to telephone a client, The New Ideas Group, Helen House, Chalbury, Kent, with vital information about a new product for which they were delaying manufacture. Unfortunately, the client's telephone system has broken down so you have to send an immediate telex message.

a Prepare the message, referring to "special steel fitments" and stating also the reason why you could not telephone as promised. Be concise.

b Send a confirmatory letter.

Check your success

Does the message explain the situation clearly and concisely? ☐

Does the confirmatory letter explain the situation in more detail? ☐

Does the letter show clearly but sensitively that the fault did not lie with you? ☐

Does the letter finish positively, by looking forward to future business co-operation? ☐

21 Advertisements

Understand how to write the text for an advertisement, with an appropriate balance between information and persuasion.

The PEI Intermediate examination sometimes includes a question involving the writing of an advertisement. It is important to remember that you should write only the text of an advertisement, and should not try to provide illustrations.

The text should be factually informative, and should also stress the **appeal** or **advantages** of the product advertised. Ideally it will have a balance between **information** and **persuasion**, but with the element of persuasion remaining unobtrusive.

Example

> APEX OFFICE SERVICES can meet most of your office needs. APEX provides **word processing, mailing, telephone answering, telex** and **accounting** services for the modern small business.
>
> Using only state of the art equipment, our experienced and professional staff will add an extra dimension to the quality and efficiency of your business, for rates as low as £10.00 per hour.
>
> Contact APEX on 803.5471 for more details.

The bulk of the 66 words in this small advertisement are used simply to **explain** the services which APEX is offering. But phrases like 'state of the art', 'experienced and professional staff', 'extra dimension to quality and efficiency' also **persuade** the reader.

Test your competence

1 Write an advertisement of no more than 50 words for the classified advertising column of a national newspaper, to advertise the Life Assurance services of Golden Age Insurance Limited. Stress that Golden Age specialises in life insurance for people of 45 years and over, that the company does not employ sales personnel, and can therefore keep its annual premiums very low. Insurance of people with a poor medical history is a speciality.

2 Write an advertisement for Penton Marina, Kuala Lumpur, Malaysia (Tel 01265 – 473826) who wish to promote Company Days on their Ocean Motor Cruiser. A group of up to 100 people can cruise on the cruiser with drinks and a quality buffet lunch for 40 dollars per head. Stress the novelty and relaxation of the cruise as a form of company entertainment. (Maximum 75 words)

Practice from the paper

Write an advertisement to be inserted in the Jolly Holidays Guide about the Golden Sands Hotel, Cliff Walk, Torquay. Mention its position, number of rooms, prices etc. The advertisement should contain not more than 35 words.

Check your success

Is the text factually informative? ☐

Does the wording suggest appeal, and attract a reader? ☐

Is persuasion unobstructive and controlled? ☐

22 Testimonials

Understand the purpose of testimonials and the style of writing that should be adopted.

A testimonial is a statement written by an employer about an employee. It is a guide to the abilities, work performance and general character and attributes of the person concerned. Testimonials are read by employers who are considering making an appointment, and who need the opinion of a previous employer on the suitability of a candidate for a job.

Testimonials are different from references. A standard testimonial may be produced by an employer and sent to a number of enquirers, whereas a reference is produced in response to a specific individual request.

A testimonial usually opens with an explanation of the work performance of an employee, and proceeds to describe the personality and interests of the person concerned.

Example

```
                TESTIMONIAL:  MRS SHARON NELSON

Sharon Nelson has worked as a Receptionist/Typist at
Debenham Brothers since September 19-.  She has always
discharged her duties with energy and a keen sense of the
company's interests.  She has a typing speed of 65 words
per minute, and is accurate and efficient in her work.  Her
spoken manner, in both face to face and telephone
conversations, is excellent, and she projects exactly the
polished and professional image that we need.  She is
always punctual and presentable, and is an admirable
receptionist.

Mrs Nelson is a sociable person and relates well to other
staff in the office.  Although hard working, she has a
pleasant sense of humour and is valued by her colleagues.
In her spare time, she plays netball for the company, and
is an active member of her local church.

I can warmly recommend Mrs Nelson as someone who will be an
asset to any organisation she joins.



M Khan

Staff Manager   5 May 19-
```

Test your competence

1 Write a testimonial for Delroy McMaster, who has worked as a Commercial Artist for your firm for four years. He has applied to be Senior Commercial Designer for Inkblot Graphics Ltd of 15 Marshland Lane, Mansfield, NOTTS. Recommend him as a hardworking designer with original ideas, and state two points in his favour.

2 Write a testimonial for Daphne Gomes who has been Head Chambermaid at The Caribbean Hotel, Port of Spain, Trinidad for the past five years. She has applied to be Manager of Domestic Services on the cruise liner SS Victoria, owned by Global Travel, 55 Progress House, Nassau, Bahamas. Recommend her as an honest person, who is hardworking and is able to organise others and work well under pressure. State two more points in her favour.

Practice from the paper

Write a testimonial to be signed by your Director concerning Jim Travers, who has worked for your firm for twelve years. He started as an office boy and by obtaining necessary qualifications, he attained a position as Chief Cashier. He has applied for a similar post in a larger firm: Life Assurance Ltd, High Street, Westham, London E2 3JK. Recommend him as a reliable and efficient member of your staff. Mention two other qualities in his favour.

Check your success

Does the testimonial describe

- The period of time Jim Travers has spent in your firm? ☐
- His career progress in that time? ☐
- His current job title and work responsibilities? ☐
- His general character and attributes? ☐
- Other qualities in his favour? ☐

23 Types of personal letter

Write personal letters using the appropriate style and tone for each type.

A personal letter is a letter written by an individual from a private address, rather than by someone writing in an official capacity on behalf of a company or organisation.

However, many personal letters are business letters in that they are sent to companies or organisations by individuals. Letters of complaint about faulty goods are an example.

Examples

```
                                        5 Hadrian Street
                                        LONDON SE10 9HP
                                        15 May 19-

Customer Service Dept
Marrat's Shoes plc
Northampton
Northants

Dear Sirs

I bought the enclosed shoes for my nine-year-old daughter in
your Woolwich store last Friday, 6 May (I enclose a dated
receipt).

As you see, the buckle strap is already broken, within twelve
days of purchase.

Please replace the shoes and refund my postage.

Thank you.

Yours faithfully

G. Spells

Mrs Gwen Spells
```

A second type of personal letter, written by one individual to another, has a social purpose. This type of letter varies substantially from business letter format, as follows.

>   86 The Drive
>   Gosforth
>   Northumberland
>
>   15.9.-

Dear Mike

I am writing to let you know that, following your excellent and very kind help to me with my work in Economics, I passed both my Stage One exams!

I am absolutely delighted, and very grateful to you.

I am now taking a two week holiday in Greece, before returning to the new term at the Polytechnic next month.

I'm really very grateful for all the time you gave up to help me, and I hope that you and the family will come up to visit me some-time this term, perhaps one Sunday when I can give you some lunch and a tour of the town.

Thanks again, and warmest regards.

[signature]

Janice

Note:
- a personal letter carries no addressee, and no reference coding
- the subscription is often less formal than a business letter, and the subscription 'Yours faithfully' is never used.
- the tone is often warm and relaxed.
- The organisation need not be quite as orderly and systematic as a business letter, but may reflect the writer's feelings directly. In the above example, for instance, Janice expresses her gratitude three different times.

Test your competence

Write the following personal letters:

1 Your ten-year-old son has developed an illness and will be unable to go on the adventure holiday you have booked for him. Write to Adventure Holidays plc, 25 Conduit Street, London WC1 PLZ to advise them of the cancellation. Give the dates of the holiday, and request a refund.

2 Your 80-year-old disabled grandmother has arrived in Jamaica after a flight from London, on which she was unaccompanied. Write a letter to Air Jamaica, 82 Lower Regent Street, London WC1 3RF to thank them for their high standard of passenger care and, in particular, the provision of a wheelchair and courier from the moment your grandmother arrived at Gatwick Airport, until she boarded the flight two hours later.

3 A friend of yours has passed an important examination at the second attempt, and will now progress to university. Write a letter to your friend, offering congratulations and some advice on how to prepare for the transition to university life.

Practice from the paper

Write a personal letter to Buy-by-Post Ltd, a mail-order firm you first wrote to a month ago. You ordered a suit as advertised in a newspaper — give details. As you enclosed a cheque (give number and date), but have not received the garment, enquire whether your order was received and if so, when you may expect to receive the goods.

Check your success

Is the letter correctly set out, with

    Address ☐

    Addressees ☐

    Date ☐

    Salutation ☐

    Subscription? ☐

Does the letter include all necessary details, such as

    Details of suit ☐

    Date of dispatch of order ☐

    Cheque number and date? ☐

Is the tone controlled and formal, as it is written to a business organisation? ☐

24 Intermediate examination questions

There now follow two **Intermediate** Examination Papers, the first of which has been worked through and solutions provided.

You are recommended to work through the first paper yourself before comparing your printouts with the solutions provided. In addition, a commentary has been provided to help you when assessing your answers.

The paper without model answers may be used for timed practice on either individual questions or the paper as a whole.

ENGLISH FOR BUSINESS COMMUNICATIONS
INTERMEDIATE

No 230 EBC

PITMAN EXAMINATIONS INSTITUTE

This paper must be returned with the candidate's work, otherwise the entry will be void and no result will be issued.

CANDIDATE'S NAME ....
(Block letters please)

CENTRE NO .... DATE ....

Time allowed: <u>2 HOURS 30 MINUTES</u>.

Answer Questions 1 and 2 and <u>THREE</u> others.

All your answers must be written in <u>ink</u>.

Ensure that your name is written clearly at the top of each of your answer sheets.

Provide suitable names and addresses when required.

---

1. You are an agent for a mail order firm. You collect money every week and pay it into the bank account. However, you have been away for two weeks on holiday and the payments have fallen behind. You receive a letter from the mail order firm saying that they have not received payments for three weeks. Write a letter in reply to this explaining what has happened and what you intend to do.

   (26 marks)

2. You have been asked to investigate the possibilities of introducing a word processing machine into the office. Write a report recommending why this should be done and what advantages there would be for the business if a word processor were introduced.

   (26 marks)

3. The firm for whom you work is having a new telephone exchange installed so as to keep in communication with its many branches. Write a memorandum from the Company Director to the supervisor of the typing pool asking him/her to recommend three or four candidates who might be willing to train as operators for the new telephone exchange. Candidates must have good speaking voices, be familiar with the organisation of the firm and willing to sit for long periods at a time. It is intended to train two operators who can work on a rota system between 8 am and 6 pm. Ask for the names to be given in within the next seven days.

   (16 marks)

(continued over)

© Sir Isaac Pitman Ltd. 1989   F/HH/DMP

Intermediate examination questions   85

4   Your company wishes to design a new letter-head. Design a suitable heading to include:

   name of firm;
   address;
   names of two directors;
   telephone number and telex.

   (16 marks)

5   Write a memorandum from the Chief Accountant to the Sales Manager: one of your customers, R D Green and Company, has not paid its account for three months. Instruct the Sales Manager not to allow further credit until the account has been paid in full. When this has been done you will notify him immediately.

   (16 marks)

6   Write a circular letter to be sent to all your customers informing them of a special sale to be held for one week (give dates). It is necessary to clear old stock in order to make room for new editions. Suggest a few titles which will be of special interest to your clients.

   (16 marks)

7   You have seen an advertisement for a personal secretary to the Managing Director of Bright New Woollens plc, a manufacturing firm in your town. Write a letter of application giving your reason for applying and enclosing details of your education, qualifications and experience, etc.

   (16 marks)

ENGLISH FOR BUSINESS COMMUNICATIONS

INTERMEDIATE

This paper must be returned with the candidate's work, otherwise the entry will be void and no result will be issued.

No. 233 EBC

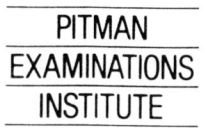

PITMAN EXAMINATIONS INSTITUTE

CANDIDATE'S NAME ....
(Block letters please)

CENTRE NO .... DATE ....

Time allowed: 2½ hours.

Answer Questions 1 and 2 and THREE others.

All your answers must be written in ink.

Ensure that your name is written clearly at the top of each of your answer sheets.

Provide suitable names and addresses when required.

---

1. Write a letter from the Rest Assured Insurance Company, 90 Leygreen Road, Croyfield, Yorkshire, CR3 YR7, informing them that from the 1 September next the firm will be providing Private Medical Care for all staff. The staff will be able to get quick treatment with no painful delays waiting to see consultants. The firm will benefit because staff will not be away from work for as long as they would have been - in the past staff had been away for weeks in pain waiting for hospital beds. Prior to the starting date in September all members of staff will have to undergo a medical - this will be with the firm's doctor. Any existing medical problems have to be revealed.

    The letter is to be signed by the Managing Director, Mr James Ambrose, and should be written in a reassuring way.

    (26 marks)

2. Report from the Training Officer of Priority Finance Ltd to the Managing Director on the advisability of bringing in specialist instructors to train staff on the new computers that are to be introduced into the firm within the next three months. The following notes are to be used:

    Many staff anxious about introduction of computers - firm supplying the computers have trained instructors who give on-site training - this scheme is now well established and has operated with success in a number of local firms - follow-up training is given at their headquarters for any staff who feel they need extra time - initial training scheme lasts for three days.

    Firm's own existing computer staff could do the training but this would divert them from the work they are currently engaged in.

    (26 marks)

    (continued over)

© Sir Isaac Pitman Ltd. 1988

F/HH/DMP

3   You work in the office of a large comprehensive school. Prepare a memorandum to be put on the Senior Teacher's notice-board for the attention of All Female Members of Staff. In recent weeks it has been noticed that an increasing number of 4th and 5th Year girls have been smoking during the morning and afternoon breaks. Special diligence is requested in the area of the Senior Girls Cloakroom and also in any other possible hidden areas. Any pupils found smoking during the next two weeks - give dates - are to be taken to Mrs Ellis, Senior Teacher's Office. Stress the urgency of this request.

(16 marks)

4   Prepare a notice to be displayed on the Staff Notice-board of Corrugated Cartons Ltd, giving details of a First Aid Course which is to be arranged for all interested staff. This should include dates, venue, times etc. A maximum of 35 words is allowed.

(16 marks)

5   You recently purchased a new television set from a Mail Order firm but it is already causing problems. When it is switched on a high-pitched whine is heard for about 15 minutes. Write a letter to Vision and Sound Mail Order, 67A Highgrove, Bromwood, Kent, BR6 RG9, giving details of the set, when it was purchased and the problem you are now experiencing. You also need to know how to get the set back to them.

(16 marks)

6   You are an international long distance lorry driver and your vehicle has broken down in Greece. Send an international telegram to your firm, Speedyfreight Ltd, explaining the situation. You do not expect to be able to return for at least a week as difficulties have been experienced in obtaining the parts needed to do the repairs. You are staying at Hotel Splendide, Athens and urgently need extra funds sent to you.

Send a letter of confirmation giving additional details of what has happened.

(16 marks)

7   Write a short report from the Personnel Officer of Home Decor Ltd to the Managing Director outlining the proposed junior recruitment campaign to be held in three local comprehensive schools.

20 new juniors are needed in late summer (August/September) - half of these on management scheme and the remainder on shop floor doing a variety of craft related jobs. Management trainees need good qualifications (specify) but the others need an ability to work with their hands. Emphasise the firm's good points - expanding and go-ahead, looks after staff well etc.

(16 marks)

Worked solutions 1

48 Kingsman Drive
London SE18 9GH

Tel 081 345 8529

14 August 19-

Mercury Mail Order Ltd
PO Box 571
Leeds LS5 4RF

Your ref: PF/JDF: AC 496

Dear Sirs

<u>AGENT 496: ACCOUNT</u>

Thank you for your letter of 19 August regarding the late payment of weekly monies into the above account for the last week of July and the first two weeks of August this year.

The explanation for the non payment is that I have been away on holiday betseen the dates of 25 July and 10 August, and did not therefore make any collections on your behalf during this time.

When I returned to collection operations on 11 August, I collected payments for the weeks of my holiday, in addition to the week of 11 August itself.

Accordingly, when I submit my accounts at the end of the current week, you will find that the monies overdue to you for my holiday period have been collected, and will total four weeks of collections.

As you have written to me over this issue, I would be glad if you will also confirm in writing that my account is fully in order for July and August. I would also inform you that I do not plan to take further holidays this year.

I look forward to receiving your confirmation.

Yours faithfully

J. Beale

Sandra Beale
Agent

Commentary

1 The letter is written with tact and control. The writer never suggests that the mail order company has made an unreasonable complaint, but explains with controlled clarity the background to the situation.

2 The tone is carefully varied. It begins with careful explanation, and then becomes more positive in requesting a confirmation that all is in order from the company.

3 The structure of the letter is deliberate and orderly. The first paragraph is purely introductory, after which the main body of the letter provides a fully detailed explanation. The letter then closes with a request for confirmation, and a clarification of future arrangements.

2

TERMS OF REFERENCE:

To investigate the possibilities of introducing a word processor into the office, and to report to Mrs H Hawkerson, Office Manager.

PROCEDURE: A study was made of existing office equipment and methods. These were compared with our neighbouring Bridgetown office, which has had word processing facilities for 2 years.

FINDINGS:

1. A word processor offers several clear advantages for a small office such as ours, when compared with the use of typewriters:

i) Word processing equipment is quieter than typewriters and therefore less disruptive to other office staff.

ii) The memory system in word processors enables similar types of letter and document to be produced extremely quickly. For example, standard contracts and agreements can be kept on disk, with minor amendments made in individual cases before printing. This saves time and paper compared with a typewriting system.

iii) Word processors enable the speedy correction of errors and can create a highly professional finish if used with a high quality printer. If, for example, a laser printer is used, results are more professional and impressive than can ever be produced by typewriter.

iv) The facility of storing material in files on disk as opposed to hard copy files in filing cabinets means a significant saving in office space.

v) Word processors with memory have the capacity to print large numbers of documents in series, with minor amendments, such as names and addresses on letters, invoice code numbers etc. For large scale clerical jobs, they can make great savings in time and labour costs.

vii) Modern secretaries are trained in word processing and are unlikely to be satisfied with typewriters, which they will regard as old-fashioned. We therefore can only keep top quality staff if we have word processors.

2. Word processing equipment is more expensive than typewriting equipment, though maintenance costs may be lower.

CONCLUSION:

The advantages of word processing are overwhelming, and the office should adopt a word processing system.

Caroline Hartley   23 February 19-

Commentary

1 The report is split into clear sections: Terms of Reference, Procedure, Findings, Conclusion.

2 Points are grouped under headed sub sections for ease of reading.

3 Use is made of two forms of numbering, in order to show main points and sub sections to points respectively.

4 The report is clearly expressed and concise.

5 The report is signed and dated.

3

MEMORANDUM

To: Typing Pool Supervisor   Date: 23/6/-

From: G Taylor (Director)

Subject: OPERATIONS FOR NEW TELEPHONE EXCHANGE

As you know, we are in the process of having a new telephone exchange installed, which will shortly require at least two new operators.

I would be very glad if you could notify me of anyone in your division who would, in your view, be suitable for these posts.

The new telephone operators must have the following qualities:

i)   A good speaking voice
ii) A firm understanding of the organisation of the company
iii) The ability to sit at a switchboard for long periods, without loss of working efficiency.

Finally, it is important to note that the new operators will have to work on a rota system, between the hours of 8.00am and 6.00pm.

Please let me have names of suitable candidates by 30/6/- at the latest.

GT

Commentary

1 The memo is concise and brief. It dispenses with the formalities of a letter, such as reference, addressee, salutation and subscription. It presents an efficient internal message with the minimum of wording.

2 By using a list of attributes for the new telephone operators, the writer of the memo presents the separate skills of the job in an effective and memorable way.

3 The tone is neutral, but respectful towards the reader.

4

£££££ SATURN SOFTWARE LIMITED £££££

Computer Programs for Modern Companies
Directors: P H Virani, C F Patel

HEAD OFFICE: 15, Snape Road, Bovingly
Tel: (0347) 34561 / 34562 Telex: 4785

Commentary

1 The letterhead provides all necessary information.

2 The letterhead is presented in a symmetrical and orderly way.

3 The letterhead projects a straightforward and professional image.

4 The spacing in the letterhead differentiates its two main sections: information about the company, its purposes and directors in the first section, and address and telecommunications details in the second section.

5 The letterhead is concise and clear.

5

MEMORANDUM

To: DENNIS GOONTING (Sales Manager)   Date: 12.6.-

From: Sharon King (Chief Accountant)

Subject: <u>OVERDUE ACCOUNT: R D GREEN AND COMPANY</u>

This customer now has an overdue account of three months standing, and has not replied to any of our standard reminder letters for payment.

In the circumstances, we must allow no further credit until the account has been paid in full.

I will immediately notify of any payment, and enable you to resume sales to Green and Co as soon as possible. But until this time please ensure that no further credit is granted.

SK

Commentary

1 The memo is brief and to the point. As it is an internal communication from one member of staff to another, salutation and subscription are not necessary, and the main point is addressed immediately.

2 The layout of the memo is simple, and makes use of normal headings.

3 In order to guarantee the success of the message, the main point (that credit must not be provided) is made twice.

4 The memo is initialled by the sender to confirm the sender's personal responsibility for its contents.

6

Barkleys and Co
46–57 Kowloon Road,
Hong Kong
Telephone: 56429 Telex 6793

25 July 19–

To all customers

Dear Customer

<u>SUMMER SALE 19-</u>

We have done it again! Barkleys is able to bring you the benefits of its great summer sale for the fourth year running. The sale will begin on Monday 9 August and finish on 16 August at 6.00pm

As always, we simply have to clear our existing stock at very low prices in order to make room for the exciting autumn book titles which will be gracing our shelves in September.

So here are some of the bargains you could collect in the sale:

<u>The Fishermen's Song by Rebecca Ford</u>

The classic romance set in a Vietnamese fishing village, with the Vietnam War as the backdrop to the tale involving an American soldier and a local family. This book has sold 50 000 copies and is reduced from 30 dollars to 9 dollars.

<u>Classic World Atlas</u>

A full colour 180-page guide to the countries and oceans of the world. Something that every family needs for basic education and an understanding of the modern world. A superb investment for your family, reduced from 60 dollars to 37.50 dollars.

<u>Vegetable Recipes of the World</u>

A book that will help you keep up with the modern trend to vegetarian food, and which will keep your health high and your food bills low. All recipes are simply explained. Reduced from 35 dollars to only 10 dollars.

Of course, these titles are only a sample. Come and see for yourself, and get the book bargain of the year at Barkleys' summer sale. We really do value your custom.

Yours sincerely

Nelson Yip
Nelson Yip
Sales Manager

Commentary

1 The letter opens with an energetic first sentence, to capture the reader's attention.

2 The bulk of the letter tries to present attractive bargains to varied types of taste and reader.

3 The letter is balanced between formal business tone and enthusiastic marketing tone.

4 The letter conveys a lot of information clearly and effectively by the use of sections and paragraphs.

5 The layout of the letter is formal and recognisable.

7

Flat 24, New Court
Hill Road
Danbury
Essex CH5 1RF

Tel: 0853 6759

The Managing Director
Bright New Woollens plc
Unit 5, Progress Estate
Danbury, Essex CH4 3RF

3 December 19-

Dear Sir

<u>VACANCY FOR PERSONAL SECRETARY</u>

I would like to apply for the above vacancy, as advertised in the 'Danbury Chronicle' on 28 November.

I am twenty-four years old, and moved to Danbury earlier this year after spending five years as a secretary with a textile firm in Bradford, Yorkshire.

I left school in 19- with GCSE passes in English, Mathematics, French and Art, and also with an RSA Stage One pass in Typing. Since then I have worked as a secretary.

I am particularly interested in continuing my career in the textile industry and have experience of dealing with both suppliers of raw wool and purchasers from major garment companies. My previous firm, Northern Textiles Ltd, will certainly remember me, and my employer, Mr H Morgan, Production Manager, will be able to provide a reference.

I am familiar with modern word processing systems and am also experienced in the operation of facsimile and telex machines. On several occasions I have travelled abroad as part of a business group, and am able to speak French and some German.

In my spare time I play squash, attend evening classes in modern languages, and visit the cinema.

I would very much welcome the chance to visit your company for an interivew, and look forward to hearing from you.

Yours faithfully

Foroza Matthews

Foroza Matthews

Commentary

1 The letter is formally written and set out, and projects an impression of professionalism and competence.

2 The writer emphasises her experience in the textile industry, and the range of her work capability.

3 The letter uses paragraphing to differentiate the varied aspects of the subject: personal background, work experience, education, leisure interests.

4 While the writer tries to present her positive qualities, the tone is suitably controlled. The letter never appears conceited or self centred.

Part 3   **Advanced**

Syllabus

English for Business Communications Advanced

(Time allowed – 3 hours)

At this stage candidates will be required to answer 5 questions, 3 of which will be compulsory: a letter, a report and an exercise in composing a concise text, eg international telegram, notice, or advertisement, plus 2 further questions from a choice of 4.

Candidates for the Advanced examination will be expected to compose correspondence from a minimum of given information. They must have a knowledge of the Intermediate Syllabus and be able to deal with other similar matters coming within the scope of general business. A higher standard of composition will be expected, however, and the matters dealt with will be of a more advanced nature and relate to a wider range of business undertakings.

They will require a fluent command of English, and sufficient office knowledge to enable them to expand notes into clear concise language, adding all necessary details to provide authentic and realistic answers. They also need to show ability to extract salient parts from a passage.

Checklist – Advanced

Aided Date Unaided Date

25 Business letters
Write a business letter showing the ability to produce and organise significant amounts of information, and to express written material in an effective and appropriate tone or range of tones.

26 Formal reports
Write a formal report from a minimal amount of information, ensuring that any conclusions/recommendations follow on logically from the information given.

27 Concise text (telex/telegram/advertisement)
Write text concisely and in an appropriate style, yet which conveys adequate information and makes effective use of headings and layout and generates interest/enthusiasm as appropriate.

28 Optional questions
Develop your writing skills with effective use of control and variation of control in all types of written communication.

29 Summary
Demonstrate the skills required in summarising material into a shorter form, yet retain and convey all the necessary information.

30 Advanced Examination Questions

Instructions for Part 3

The Pitman English for Business Communication series of examinations is designed as an inter-related group of awards, which develop and assess levels of skill at the three different, but related levels of Elementary, Intermediate and Advanced. It therefore follows that the best way to prepare for the Advanced examination is to study thoroughly first the Elementary, and then the Intermediate examination topics. This will provide a grounding in the theoretical and practical aspects on which the Advanced examination is based.

The distinctive feature of the Advanced examination is given in a single sentence from the syllabus:

> 'Candidates for the Advanced examination will be expected to compose correspondence from a minimum of given information.'

Although the questions in the Advanced examination may look similar to those at Intermediate level, the answers will be very different. They will be longer, more fully developed, independent responses to the examination question. You will therefore need to be able to **compose**, **develop** and **organise** longer and more involved pieces of writing than at either Intermediate or Elementary level.

The Advanced paper itself consists of five questions, in a three hour examination. This longer time allowance reflects the need to develop answers at greater length than in the other examinations. The first three questions are compulsory, and consist of a business letter, a formal report and a concise text (such as an international telegram, an advertisement or a notice). The examination topics show a strong similarity with the Intermediate examination. Following the compulsory questions, candidates choose two further questions, which take the form of memoranda, letters, reports or a summary of main points from a passage of writing. The summary is the only exercise which arises only at Advanced level. This exercise will therefore be covered at length in the following units.

It is worth stressing that success in the Advanced examination depends more on the ability to provide **full** and **detailed** treatment of question material than on the learning of a large body of theory, beyond that learned for the Elementary and Intermediate examinations.

For this reason, this section comprises largely discussion of detailed and extensive treatment of individual questions on the following topics:

Business letters
Formal reports
Telexes/Telegrams/Advertisements

Memoranda
Personal letters
Selection and summary

In addition, Part 3 of this guide is organised slightly differently from earlier units. To enable the reader to focus on the treatment of individual examination questions, and on the need for detailed development of answers, it proceeds by treating each of the compulsory topics (Business letters, Formal reports and Concise texts) in four stages as follows:
- Example (question)
- Worked example (model answer)
- Commentary
- Practice from the paper
- Check your success

The chapter concludes with general advice on the other question areas (memos, letters and reports) and with a section on **summary**.

25 Business letters

Write business letters showing the ability to produce and organise significant amounts of information, and to express written material in an effective and appropriate tone or range of tones.

A letter writing technique suitable for Advanced level can best be demonstrated by a worked example from a question typical of a PEI Advanced level examination question.

Example

Write a letter to a Mail Order company, to whom you sent two separate orders on successive days, four weeks ago. You have not received the goods, nor any acknowledgement. Give all necessary details to help them trace the order, and state whether you still require the goods.

Worked example

```
                                              55 Beech Grove
                                              Standerley
                                              GLOS GL6 4RH

                                              Tel: 0583 38541

     Complaints Department
     Harris and Williams Ltd
     4-12 The Rise
     Peterborough
     PB3 6YJ                                  21 November 19-

     Dear Sirs

                    OVERDUE ORDERS NOS 545/S, 545/T
                    -------------------------------

     I am writing to complain about your failure to provide prompt
     delivery of the above orders, and to enquire about the prospects
     for delivery in the near future.

     The two orders were both placed by post.  The first order, which you
     coded 545/S, was for a tubular steel bunk bed and mattress set,
     priced at £149.95 inclusive of delivery.  This was ordered on 11
     October this year.  On 15 October, I received a confirmation of the
     order, but have heard nothing further.  My cheque in payment has
     been accepted and processed by yourselves, and the funds were
     cleared from my bank account on 17 October.

     The second order, which you coded 545/T, was for a child's garden
     swing, priced at £37.50 inclusive of delivery.  This was ordered on
     12 October, and I received a confirmation of the order on 18
     October.  The cheque enclosed in full payment has been processed,
     and funds cleared from my bank on 20 October.
```

However, despite your acceptance of the order and of the payments, neither item has yet been delivered. the delay in the arrival of the bunk bed has proved particularly inconvenient, as I have consequently had to postpone arrangements for a planned overnight visit by some friends with their childen.

Apart from the inconvenience to which I have been put, I find it strange that at no time have you attempted to contact me with an explanation or an apology.

While I still need both items ordered, I am not prepared to wait indefinitely. Please note that if you cannot deliver the items to my home by 30 November, I wish to cancel both orders and receive a full refund. As you have defaulted on your commitment to deliver promptly, I feel quite sure that I am within my rights to cancel, should delivery not occur by the end of this month.

Would you please contact me by letter or telephone immediately on receipt of this letter to explain the situation. I have used your services on many occasions, and have always been fully satisfied. I am confident that the difficulties of these two orders will be quickly resolved, and I look forward to hearing from you.

Yours sincerely

P. Bell

Mr P Bell

Commentary

This is a good example of the approach required at Advanced level for the following reasons:

1 The layout of the letter is accurate and conventional. Although it is written by a private individual from his own address, it uses features of business letter layout such as addressee and subject heading.

2 The writer has invented suitable details in order to respond **fully** to the terms of the question. These details include matters such as the order codes, the type and price of the goods, the method and details of payment and the nature of the inconvenience suffered.

3 The letter is sectioned and paragraphed usefully. It explains the details of each order in separate paragraphs, and then uses a further paragraph to explain the inconvenience caused. The fifth paragraph sets out terms for completion or cancellation, and the final paragraph closes the letter in a firm but courteous manner.

4 Tone is consistently suitable. Dissatisfaction is expressed clearly, but without aggression. The tone of the final paragraph softens slightly, in order to establish a good basis for future dealings.

The question is demanding, although brief and apparently simple. A good answer is one which has considered the four crucial areas of **content**, **layout**, **style** and **expression**.

Practice from the paper

1 Write a letter to a Mail Order firm to whom you sent an order eight weeks ago. You have not received the goods. Give all necessary details to help them trace your order. State whether you still require the goods if the order has been lost in the post.

2 Below is given an extract from a conversation overheard in a factory canteen. As secretary to the Managing Director you have brought this to his attention and he has asked you to write out a draft letter to all staff telling them that although informal discussions have taken place with an associated company and there is the possibility of a merger, it is unlikely that redundancies will arise and in fact more work is likely to result. The reason is that the company needs more money. Stress that the Managing Director will keep staff informed, they are to ignore rumours and any decisions taken will be for the best interests of the company and staff.

"Here, John, don't say I told you, but I've just heard from a friend of mine in head office that the company's going to be taken over! Well that's what I heard; big firm, Universal Electronics — so I was told. Apparently they're going to close down the Northwood factory — six hundred work there, at least. It doesn't look bright for the office staff either. Something to do with rationalisation in the industry. Anyway, I heard there's going to be a meeting of the trade union next week — the shop stewards at Northwood are pretty angry — heard nothing officially — and the people at the Oldgate factory are going to stage a sit-in the day after tomorrow. It's all over the building! Only keep it to yourself — I didn't tell you!"

3 Your firm, Golden Pottery Ltd, has received a letter from Mrs G H Driway complaining that a forty-piece dinner service (Golden Beauty) which she bought from a store in her town for £103.55 has deteriorated by use in her dishwasher, in spite of a written guarantee that it would withstand very hot water.

Reply to Mrs Driway's letter, pointing out that hers is not the first complaint; the design has been withdrawn; can choose an alternative design or wait for new production; you are writing to Manager of the store for him to make necessary arrangements; express your Managing Director's apologies for inconvenience caused.

Check your success

1 Does your letter give all necessary details, to help the tracing of the order? ☐

Does your letter explain fully why continued failure to deliver is inconvenient? ☐

Does your letter explain dissatisfaction at the extremely long delay? ☐

Does your letter state clearly whether or not you still require the goods, and a further period you will wait, prior to final cancellation of the order? ☐

2 Does your draft letter open by acknowledging that there have been rumours in the factory? ☐

Does the letter *clearly* explain that only informal talks have taken place? ☐

Does your letter clearly explain the difference between informal talks and formal agreement? ☐

Does your letter explain that, even if a takeover does take place, redundancies are not planned? ☐

Does your letter explain the reason that the company is interested in the possibility of the takeover? ☐

Does your letter stress that all staff will be kept informed, and that decisions will be in staff's best interest? ☐

3 Is your letter appropriately set out? ☐

Does your letter acknowledge:

   The high price of the dinner service ☐

   The fact that Mrs Driway has a legitimate complaint ☐

   That you accept responsibility and will replace the service? ☐

Does your letter explain that hers is not the only complaint? ☐

Does your letter explain that Golden Pottery products are generally reliable and of high quality, and that this was an unfortunate exception? ☐

Does your letter explain Mrs Driway's options? ☐

Does your letter explain the arrangements that you are making? ☐

Does your letter apologise on behalf of the Managing Director? ☐

26 Formal reports

Write a formal report from a minimal amount of information, ensuring that any conclusions/recommendations follow on logically from the information given.

The theoretical explanation of report writing provided in Unit 18 is a useful preliminary to this section, and should be read before proceeding further.

At Advanced level, a report has to be composed from a minimal amount of information in the question. It is extremely important that any conclusions and/or recommendations that you make in your answer follow logically from the information given in the question, or from any information invented by you as part of your development of the question. The report writing exercise is therefore partly a test of your ability to draw logical and useful conclusions from the information in the question.

As was explained in Unit 18, reports must be clearly and logically set out, with the use of **main headings** and **sub-headings**, and **numbered sections** and **paragraphs** where this is helpful.

Another important consideration is the ability to distinguish between **fact** and **judgement**. Matters of fact will be presented in a section headed **findings**, while the writer's judgements on those facts will be presented as **conclusions**. If the conclusions of the report imply a need for action or for a change in policy on the part of the organisation concerned, it will be appropriate to include a section on **recommendations**.

As the report is a formal document, a controlled and formal tone throughout will be necessary.

Example

Read the following Memorandum and notes and as Senior Clerk, compose the report requested by the Managing Director of your company, Leatherware Ltd.

Memorandum from Managing Director to Senior Clerk:

> 'I have recently been receiving a number of complaints from customers about staff's poor telephone manners. This is losing customers and clearly something must be done as a matter of urgency. Please look into this for me and submit a report on your findings with recommendations for improving matters.'

Worked example

REPORT ON TELEPHONE PERFORMANCE OF STAFF OF LEATHERWARE LTD

By Denis Li, Senior Clerk   Report submitted 1.9.19-

1 TERMS OF REFERENCE

To investigate the telephone manners and performance of staff throughout the organisation, and to make recommendations for urgent action which will lead to improvements. The report is for the Managing Director.

2 FINDINGS

My survey of staff telephone use revealed many problems and shortcomings. In many cases, the causes of these shortcomings were apparent. I have therefore presented my findings in two sections: Current Failings, and Causes of Failings.

(a) CURRENT FAILINGS

The principal current failings in our telephone use are as follows:

i) There are long delays in answering the telephone in many branches. These delays are caused partly by understaffing, and also by a widespread attitude that makes a telephone call a low priority. 'They will call again if it is important' was a comment that I heard frequently.

ii) Staff performance in handling the telephone for business purposes is frequently poor. The most widespread and serious weaknesses are as follows:

* Telephone enquirers often cannot obtain the information they seek, as staff lack detailed product knowledge.

* Calls are often handed from one staff member to another. This causes delay and expense for the enquirer, and projects an image of incompetence and a failure to take responsibility on our part. Branch managers are frequently unavailable to make a decision as a result of a call, or to handle a call personally when necessary.

* Calls making sales enquiries are often poorly followed up. Staff do not treat telephone callers with the same level of seriousness and courtesy that is given to a personal caller.

* Calls are not always recorded. Many telephone points have no message pads, although Stationery Stores have very large stocks. A call that is not recorded is virtually impossible to follow up.

* Staff frequently use the telephone for personal calls. This both denies the use of the telephone for business purposes, and wastes the time of the staff member making the call.

(b) CAUSES OF FAILINGS

i) Lack of training has been a major cause of our current difficulties. Since the Training Manager left six months ago, Leatherware has offered no induction training for new staff. It is clear that both induction training and in-service training for established staff would eliminate many failings. For example, the low priority given to calls, the lack of product knowledge on the part of staff, the reluctance to take full responsibility for a call, the failure to record calls and the failure to follow up calls could all be improved and possibly eliminated by an active training programme.

ii) Some of our failings are organisational. These are shown as follows:

* Training is organised on a branch to branch basis. There is no centrally controlled training, and no department ensuring that staff are equipped with telephone skills.

* The duties of our Branch Managers as currently organised take them away from their branches frequently. They are thus unable to deal with telephone enquiries, and are also unable to control and discourage personal calls by staff.

* There is no mechanism for checking the methods used by individual branches and staff members for recording and following up calls.

3 CONCLUSIONS

i) There are widespread failings in our current telephone performance, which are costly to business success.

ii) These failings are largely caused by a lack of suitable training for both new staff and for established staff.

iii) Some of the failings are caused by current aspects of our organisation.

4 RECOMMENDATIONS

i) We should immediately recruit a new Training Manager. One of their earliest priorities should be to develop telephone training courses for all staff, dealing with product knowledge, call reception and courtesy, call recording and call follow up.

ii) All Branch Managers should insist on the recording of all telephone calls on message pads, and should collect and examine messages from each telephone point on a twice daily basis.

iii) Branches should record the number of telephone message pads that are used monthly. These statistics should be returned to me.

iv) We should organise the workload of Branch Managers to enable them to spend the bulk of their time in their own branches. This will reduce the number of personal telephone calls, and improve dealings with enquiries. Deputy Managers should be appointed to carry out Manager's duties when they are unavoidably absent.

Dennis Li
Senior Clerk

Commentary

The worked example shows several of the characteristics of a well written report:

1 It is carefully organised into sections. The Findings are presented as matters of **fact**, and the writer's **judgement** on how to deal with the problems, are presented separately as **recommendations**. The sectioning of the report also makes it easy to read, follow and remember.

2 The use of **headings** and **numbered sections** and **sub sections** helps the writer to organise material clearly. For example, in the section on findings, the findings are sub-divided into sub-sections: Current Failings and Causes. Each of these sub-sections is numbered separately. The numbering system helps the clarity of the report.

3 The tone of the report is formal and unemotional.

4 Conclusions summarise the findings of the report.

5 Recommendations suggest a way forward, towards resolving the problems uncovered in the findings and summarised in the conclusions.

6 The report as a whole is clear, systematic and organised. It concludes with the signature and job title of the writer.

Practice from the paper

Your employer, the Financial Director, has asked you to investigate the possibility of leasing, instead of buying on hire purchase, the next fleet of company cars.

Using the following notes, make your report:

leasing for 2 year period at an average mileage of 15,000 per annum – £2,200 rental in advance; car delivered with road fund licence; maintenance and service, including tyres and batteries, included; vehicle returnable after two years – no depreciation; rental allowable as business expense offset against tax; company responsible for insurance

Check your success

Is the report appropriately sectioned as follows:

Terms of Reference ☐

Findings ☐

Conditions ☐

Recommendations ☐

Is tone formal and unemotional? ☐

Do conclusions summarise the findings? ☐

Are matters of judgement expressed as recommendations, and kept separate from matters of reported fact earlier in the report? ☐

27 Concise text (telex/telegram/advertisement)

Write text concisely and in an appropriate style, yet which conveys adequate information and makes effective use of headings and layout and generates interest/enthusiasm as appropriate.

This exercise at Advanced level is very similar to questions on the same topics at other levels. The points of theory covering these topics are in Units 8, 9, 20 and 21. Read through these Units before attempting the questions at Advanced level.

At this level, the ability to convey information **concisely** and in an appropriate **style** are highly important. In exercises such as the writing of an advertisement, factors of layout such as the use of headings, the layout of text into paragraphs and sections, and the ability to generate interest or enthusiasm in the reader through the use of suitable language are all important.

The requirement of the production of concise written expression is often limited to one part of the question. For example, questions frequently involve the production of a telegram or telex followed by a covering letter. In this case, the requirement for concise expression obviously applies only to the telegram or telex. The second part of the question offers you the opportunity to demonstrate to the examiner the range of your writing ability, by the production of a fuller document. While this type of two-part question also features at Intermediate level, at Advanced level you should be able to use such questions to demonstrate the ability to write effectively in both concise and more developed styles on the same topic.

Example

You are secretary to Mr E F Holdsworthy, the Assistant Export Manager, who left the office this morning en route to Scandinavia. He is due to arrive in Stockholm tomorrow evening where he is to be met by the firm's agent, Mr E Horsa, who has arranged a programme of visits for him.

You have just received a telex message from Mr Horsa's secretary, informing you that Mr Horsa has been involved in an accident and will be unable to meet Mr Holdsworthy as arranged.

Compose a radio-telegram, in not more than 15 words, to be sent to Mr Holdsworthy on board the ship to Scandinavia, telling him of the accident and asking him to telephone Mr Horsa's secretary on 01 6767 to discuss new arrangements.

In addition, write a letter to Mr Holdsworthy, who will be staying at the Central Hotel, Stockholm, asking him to let you have details of the new arrangements.

Worked example

Radio telegram message

```
HORSA NOT MEETING YOU TOMORROW  -  ACCIDENT. PLEASE TELEPHONE
SECRETARY MISS NEILSON 01 6767 FOR INSTRUCTIONS.   PAULA.
```

```
                            Scandexport Ltd
                            55 North Prospect
                                Felixstowe
                            Suffolk CH5 7YT

                            Tel: 654 376987

    Mr E F Holdsworthy (Guest)
    The Central Hotel
    Railway Square
    Stockholm  SWEDEN

    Dear Mr Holdsworthy

               NEW ARRANGEMENTS FOR VISIT TO SWEDEN
               ─────────────────────────────────────

    I am writing to confirm and to follow up on my radio telephone
    message to you on your sea journey to Scandinavia.  I assume you
    received the message, which was sent at 16.00 yesterday.

    We were advised shortly before this time by a telephone call from
    Stockholm office that Mr Horsa had slipped on an icy pavement and
    damaged a hip.  He is being kept in hospital, probably for at
    least two days.

    I therefore contacted you to notify you that he would not be
    meeting you on arrival.  Mr Horsa's secretary, Brigitte Neilson,
    asked me to notify you of the accident and to contact her office
    on arrival.  I do hope that the message reached you promptly, and
    that your arrival went smoothly, despite the accident.

    As a result of the accident, I imagine that you will need to change
    some arrangements for your visit, possibly including changes to
    dates of travel.

    When you have made the necessary plans, please advise me by
    telephone or telex, so that I can amend any travel bookings for
    your return journey, and advise other colleagues here of your
    amended programme.

    I do hope the trip goes well.  Please give Mr Horsa the best wishes
    of myself and everyone here for a speedy recovery, and please let
    me know if we can be of any help to you during your time away from
    the office.

    With best wishes for a successful trip

    Yours sincerely

    Paula Yates

    Paula Yates
    Secretary to Export Department
```

Commentary

1 The text of the telegram is extremely sparse and concise, and covers only the essential information. There is not even space for simple courtesies, as is shown by the reference to 'Horsa' instead of 'Mr Horsa'. The function of the telegram is simply to convey the basic information clearly and speedily in the minimum number of words.

2 The letter is written entirely differently. It is set out in conventional fashion, and there is clearly no pressure to economise on either space or on the number of words used.

3 The letter succeeds as a follow-up to the telegram initially because it succeeds in **confirming** and explaining **fully** the basic information of the radio telegram.

4 The letter fulfils other functions, such as indicating the need for Mr Holdsworthy to inform the UK office of his amended programme.

5 It also shows careful control of tone. It is a formal business letter, but it succeeds in projecting an air of concern, both for the injured Mr Horsa, and for Mr Holdsworthy, who has to make new arrangements. The letter is an effective, official document, while at the same time expressing a sympathetic tone.

The requirement of candidates to be **concise** in the first part of the exercise (the radio telegram), and then to demonstrate other skills in the latter part of the question (the letter) is clearly shown.

28 Optional questions

Develop your writing skills with effective use of control and variation of control in all types of written communication.

While the first three questions on the examination paper at Advanced level are compulsory, you can then choose **two** out of **four** remaining questions on the paper.

With the exception of the summary, all the skill areas tested in the optional questions at Advanced level will be familiar to any student who has studied English for Business Communication at Intermediate level.

To prepare for these optional questions, you are recommended to read the units on **memoranda**, **special types of business letter**, **testimonials** and **personal letters**. You must also remember that examiners at Advanced level, in every area of the examination paper, are keen to see you demonstrating your abilities to **develop** the questions with additional material of your own, and to show **control** and, where suitable, a **variation of tone** in your writing.

Example

You are Maintenance Manager for Dofy Ltd, a large department store in a central city location, which is understaffed and extremely busy with high levels of custom. In recent months you have had to make twelve sets of repairs to the locks on glass showcases, which are used to display jewellery and small items of clothing such as hats and scarves.

Damage has been caused to the lock mechanisms of the cases by careless opening and closing. Repairs to the locks are expensive, as parts must be specially imported.

Write a memo to all shop assistants which explains the problem and requests particular care. Point out that no special expertise is needed to use the showcases properly.

MEMORANDUM

To: ALL SHOP ASSISTANTS   Date: 5/3/-

From: MICHAEL OJAMBO, MAINTENANCE MANAGER

Subject: REPAIRS TO GLASS SHOWCASES

I am writing to ask for your help and co-operation in the care of our glass showcases. In recent months we have had to make twelve similar repairs to the lock mechanisms of these showcases.

This is because the locks are too delicate to withstand being slammed shut and wrenched open. I appreciate that shop assistants, under pressure of work and concerned to serve customers promptly, may sometimes accidentally mishandle this delicate equipment.

Repairs to the cases are very expensive, as we have to import components from Switzerland for the locks. They also take several hours to repair, which presents my staff from dealing with other equally important matters.

I recognise the great pressure under which we all work, especially those who have the burdensome job of dealing with the public.

But please try to handle our glass cases with particular care. This will be of benefit to staff and customers alike.

Thank you,

M O

Commentary

1 The memo *develops* its point well. It explains appropriate details at length, such as the exact problem with the locks, and the two particular causes of expense.

2 The tone is carefully controlled and varied and the writer is careful to show that they recognise the pressure and difficulty of this job.

3 The memo closes with a courteous request and is likely to secure the necessary care without causing any offence.

Overall, it is well developed, shows well-controlled tone, and is clear and effective.

Practice from the paper

The Head of the Secretarial Studies Department has just completed the schedules of entries for public examinations, which she has found extremely time-consuming because of the number of minor faults in the information given to her by candidates.

She has asked you to draft a memorandum which she will send to all tutors requesting their cooperation to ensure that in future candidates provide full and accurate information. Remind tutors that printed forms are available for this purpose; one form completed fully for each subject entry; each form signed by teacher approving entry; each form countersigned by Finance Officer indicating entry fee paid; tutor's responsibility to check finally.

Check your success

Is your memorandum appropriately set out to include

- To ☐
- From ☐
- Date ☐
- Subject ☐
- Initials or signature? ☐

Does it explain the loss of time caused by minor faults? ☐

Does it explain that printed forms are available? ☐

Does it convey the need for change, without offending the recipient? ☐

Is it formal and clear? ☐

Practice from the paper

For several years you have been corresponding with someone in another country who has invited you to visit them for two weeks when convenient.

Choosing any country you wish, write a letter accepting this invitation, and stating the date on which you would like to arrive. Mention also two things that you would be especially interested in doing during your visit, giving brief reasons for your choice, and ask if these can be arranged.

Check your success

Is your letter suitably set out for a personal letter, including

- Your address ☐
- The date ☐
- A suitably personal salutation ☐
- A suitably personal subscription? ☐

Does your letter include details of activities you would like to do, with reasons? ☐

Practice from the paper

You are the Senior Clerk in the General Office of Supasports Ltd, of Harbour Way, Portside, PT2 AES, wholesalers of aquatic sports equipment, and you have been asked to give your opinion of a new layout for the company's headed paper.

Optional questions 113

Write a memorandum to the Manager of the Reprographic Department, giving your suggestions for the use of colour in the design, with an estimate of the cost of production for 10,000 copies. You do not think that the design at present adequately represents the firm's image. You wish to make an appointment to discuss the matter. This must be done before any final decision is made.

Check your success

Is your memo appropriately set out to include

- To ☐
- From ☐
- Date ☐
- Subject ☐
- Initials or signature? ☐

Are your objections to the present design clearly and fully explained? ☐

Is your request for a meeting presented forcefully and courteously? ☐

29 Summary

Demonstrate the skills required in summarising material into a shorter form, yet retain and convey all the necessary information.

The summary exercise appears only on the Advanced paper.

Summary is an exercise that appears in many courses and examinations. It is a frequently used and extremely important skill in business, and many executives and managers spend time reading and summarising material into shorter form for their seniors to read.

The summary in the examination is an exercise that has to be completed in approximately 30 to 35 minutes. With this suggested time allocation in mind, the following procedure is suggested

1 Read and re-read the passage. (5 minutes)

2 Study the wording of the question to determine the purpose of your final summary. This will help you to select and omit material appropriately. (2 minutes)

3 Read the passage a third time and underline the main points. List these main points. (3 minutes)

4 Write up your list of main points, taking care to **avoid repetition**. Also check that you have excluded any unnecessary **illustrations**, **examples** and **minor details**. (10 minutes)

5 Count the number of words in your passage, and amend it according to the word limit, if one is set. Write out your final version of the answer. (10 minutes)

6 Make a final check of your work. (5 minutes.)

Example

Your employer, a car manufacturer, is due to speak to the Car Users' Association on the most economical use of petrol.

He has written out his speech below, but has now asked you to make headings and brief notes of the most important points – also to supply a main heading:

With today's high petrol prices and the overall cost of running a car, it is useful to know a few simple tips on how to get maximum mileage out of a gallon of petrol. Use as little choke as possible. The use of choke is especially needed on cold mornings to stop the car from 'coughing'. Never warm up an engine whilst stationary – get moving as soon as possible and use journey to warm up engine. In cold weather it is advisable to blank off radiator for short journeys. However, this depends on the type of cooling system in your car, eg transverse engine difficult to blank off. Use accelerator lightly to build up speed through the gears and when in top gear increase speed gently. Remember, too high a speed gobbles petrol. Brakes use petrol by destroying momentum of the car so, apart from emergencies, ease off brakes when approaching bends, traffic lights, hold-ups, etc. If you are in a long hold-up it is best to switch off engine. Correct pressure is important as under-inflated tyres use petrol. Tyre pressure should be checked at a garage regularly. Binding brakes cause friction and increase petrol consumption. Point gaps should be checked and corrected every 2,000 miles or so. The contact breaker gap should be checked every 1,000 miles as these become burned and pitted. All these points outline the main ways for getting maximum petrol economy so be sure to treat your car gently and keep it in perfect running order. Follow them carefully and pay fewer visits to the petrol pumps!

Worked example

```
                        FUEL ECONOMY FOR THE MOTORIST
                        ─────────────────────────────

        Techniques for achieving fuel economy fall into two main
        categories. Driving for Economy, and Maintenace for Economy.

        DRIVING FOR ECONOMY
        ───────────────────

        When starting car, use the choke as little as possible. (Choke is
        expensive on fuel).

        Once engine is going, get the car moving: switch off if in a long
        hold-up.  (Wasteful to run engine while car is stationary.)

        Drive steadily, with moderate use of accelerator and brakes:
        maintain momentum.  (Undue use of accelerator or brakes wastes
        fuel.)

        MAINTENANCE FOR ECONOMY
        ───────────────────────

        Blank off radiator for short journeys, if this can be done easily.
        (Hotter engine will give better economy.)

        Keep tyre pressures at correct levels.  Under-inflated tyres cause
        excessive petrol consumption.)

        Check efficiency of brakes, and avoid binding brakes.  (Excessive
        petrol consumption.)

        Make regular checks on points and contact breaker gaps.  (Engine
        efficiency will improve fuel consumption.)
```

Commentary

1 The decision about what to leave out is helped by a consideration of **purpose**. As the talk is on fuel economy, all the material is organised with this topic in mind.

2 The summary is helped by **categorising** the points into two main sections: a section on driving, and a section on maintenance. These categories help the writer to organise the summary in a clear and comprehensive way.

3 As the question asks for notes on a speech, many of the main points are supported with a brief explanation in brackets. This enables the speaker to **illustrate** and **develop** the point that they are making.

4 The summary avoids repetition. Although many of the points are similar, no single point is repeated.

5 The main heading prepares the audience for the material which follows, and provides a central focal subject to which each individual point is directed.

6 While the summary is clear, it is brief, written in note form, and does not waste words.

Practice from the paper

Yesterday a consignment of spare parts for Machine No LX 259 was despatched from Make & Mend Ltd, to Looms & Tools Ltd, by Overland Transport. This morning it was discovered that a small box containing 100 screws had been left out of the packing case. It was immediately posted to the consignee by air mail.

a) Compose an international telegram to the consignee in not more than 15 words, explaining what has happened.

b) Confirm the international telegram by letter.

Check your success

Is your telegram clear and concise? ☐

Is the follow-up letter appropriately set out? ☐

Does the follow up letter

  Explain the omission ☐

  Explain how the omission arose ☐

  Give details of the time and date of the dispatch of the missing screws ☐

  Apologise for the omission? ☐

Practice from the paper

As Installation Manager for your company, Advanced Business Systems Ltd, you recently arrived in West Africa to install a new computer for the

National Bank. You are staying at the Natira Plaza Hotel, Main Street, Natiraville. On installing the computer, you found that a vital piece of equipment, coded XCV/224/6P/WX, was missing from the air-freighted crates. It is essential that the computer is installed within seven days, or the bank's accounting procedures will be seriously affected. Compose a telegram to your firm asking for the piece of equipment to be delivered as a matter of urgency. Then write a letter to your company outlining the situation more fully and requesting that a sum of £300 is cabled to you to cover the expenses of a longer stay. If the equipment arrives in time, you expect to be in West Africa a further 14 days.

Check your success

Does the telegram:
Explain the urgent need for the piece of equipment in clear concise terms? ☐

Give the number of the part needed? ☐

Stress the urgency of the situation? ☐

Does the letter
Explain the omission situation fully ☐

Request extra money ☐

Give details of likely time scale if part arrives in time ☐

Stress urgent need for part ☐

Explain that prompt delivery is in everyone's interest? ☐

Practice from the paper

You have received an urgent telephone message from the Despatch Department, telling you that they have, by mistake, sent a consignment of a dangerous liquid to a customer, instead of paint.

Write a telegram, using not more than 15 words, to the customer, John Lines & Co, warning them of the possible danger and asking them to keep the consignment for collection by your firm's van.

Write a letter to confirm the telegram.

Check your success

Does the telegram
- Clearly explain the danger ☐
- Use concise, clear wording ☐
- Outline request to keep liquid? ☐

Does the letter
- Apologise sincerely for the mistake ☐
- Acknowledge extreme seriousness of the mistake ☐
- Explain how mistake arose ☐
- Thank John Lines and Co for their help ☐
- Make a commitment to future levels of service? ☐

Is the letter appropriately set out? ☐

Does it apologise and explain fully? ☐

30 Advanced examination questions

There now follow two **Advanced** Examination Papers, the first of which has been worked through and solutions provided.

You are advised to work through the first paper yourself before comparing your printouts with the solutions provided.

In addition, a commentary has been included to help you when assessing your answers.

The papers without model answers may be used for timed practice on either individual questions, or on the paper as a whole.

ENGLISH FOR BUSINESS COMMUNICATIONS
ADVANCED

No. 326 EBC

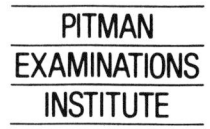

PITMAN EXAMINATIONS INSTITUTE

This paper must be returned with the candidate's work, otherwise the entry will be void and no result will be issued.

CANDIDATE'S NAME ....
(Block letters please)

CENTRE NO .... DATE ....

Time allowed: <u>3 hours</u>.

Answer Questions 1, 2 and 3 and <u>TWO</u> others.

All your answers must be written in <u>ink</u>.

Ensure that your name is written clearly at the top of each of your answer sheets.

Provide suitable names and addresses when required.

---

1. You work for a charity such as "Save the Children Fund" or "OXFAM". There is a special and urgent need in a certain part of Africa where thousands of refugees and others are without food or medical care. Draft a letter to be circulated widely in the Western World, appealing for gifts of money, food or medicines to help those in desperate need.

    You must describe the conditions and say how help can be sent and in what form, eg clothing, food, money, transport. Make an appeal to compassion and generosity.

    (20 marks)

2. You have been asked to investigate the conditions under which young employees have to work in a sewing factory. You spend several weeks alongside these young workers. Describe the conditions of work, eg number of hours, times for breaks and meals; the pay they receive; facilities available - such as canteen, sports, first aid, rest area or transport to and from work. Draw up precise conclusions as to what improvements can be made with recommendations.

    Address the report to the Managing Director.

    (20 marks)

3. Prepare an international telegram from a Sales Representative in Tokyo to the Head Office in London. He has been very successful in gaining buyers. He wishes to stay on for two more weeks and suggests another assistant salesman might join him immediately. There is a rise in the value of the yen and reduction in restrictions on imports to Japan.

    Follow this with a letter giving full details.

    (Continued)

© Sir Isaac Pitman Ltd. 1988

F/HH/DMP

Advanced examination questions 121

4 The Royal Shakespear Company at Stratford-on-Avon has published its programme for the Summer Season. There are four plays being presented at matinees and evening performances each week. Write a letter to the booking office asking for tickets for your class of eighteen.

(20 marks)

5 Write a memorandum from the Chief Accountant to the sales room staff asking them to let you have the advice notes and despatch notes more promptly, so that they can be checked with the invoices and payment be made at the end of each month.

(20 marks)

6 Write a letter of application for the following position:

John Pollard and Sons plc.

WANTED smart girl or boy to train as Personnel Officer. Applicants must have three 'O' Level passes, including English Language. Write giving full details of education, with names of two referees, to R J Williams, Company Secretary, not later than the last day of this month.

(20 marks)

7 You have been asked to set out instructions for a new employee on how to use one of the following:

(a) A Word Processor.
(b) Photocopier.
(c) Duplicating machine (state which type).

(20 marks)

```
ENGLISH FOR BUSINESS COMMUNICATIONS
           ADVANCED
```

This paper must be returned with the candidate's work, otherwise the entry will be void and no result will be issued.

No 329 EBC

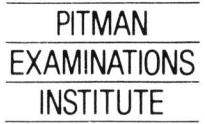

PITMAN EXAMINATIONS INSTITUTE

CANDIDATE'S NAME ....
(Block letters please)

CENTRE NO .... DATE ....

Time allowed: 3 hours.

Answer Questions 1, 2 and 3 and TWO others.

All your answers must be written in ink.

Ensure that your name is written clearly at the top of each of your answer sheets.

Provide suitable names and addresses when required.

---

1. Prepare a circular letter to be sent to all households in the town of Uxforth from the Principal of the local evening college informing them of the evening classes available from September next. The letter should urge people to think seriously about starting an evening class and should also point out that there are courses designed for those who have been away from formal education for a long time, those who want to learn a new skill, those who want to pursue a hobby and for those who want to improve their existing qualifications.

    (20 marks)

2. Write a report from the personnel officer of a large mail order company to the board of directors about the training schemes suggested for the following September when a large number of staff are expected to join the company from local schools. The report should also stress that the scheme is also for existing members of staff. It should be divided into two sections with suggested courses for existing staff and for new entrants to the firm.

    The following notes might be of help.

    Courses offered by local college - Keyboarding for Beginners.
    - Basic Word Processing.
    - Various commercial courses (specify).
    - GCSE and 'A' in a number of subjects: English, Accounts, Business Studies.

    Special rates given to firm if enough people want to attend from the firm - minimum 5 for any course.

    Courses designed and run by the firm - refresher courses in Computing, Word Processing, Audio Typing.
    Six week training course for telephonists.

    Details should be given of existing staff who might benefit from various courses especially those who have been seen as management material.

    (20 marks)

© Sir Isaac Pitman Ltd. 1988

F/HH/DMP

Advanced examination questions 123

3 Prepare an advertisement to be inserted in the local newspaper for one of the following:

(a) French teacher urgently needed for one term at local school.
(b) New driving instructor advertising for pupils.

All details are to be included - addresses, rates of pay, ages to be taught. Ensure that the correct tone is conveyed.

(20 marks)

4 Write a memorandum from the sales manager at the head office of a firm manufacturing shoes for young children, to all branch managers telling them of a training session in fitting for all new staff. Everyone has to be trained to do this properly. Give details of the venues - six in different areas of the country - dates etc.

(20 marks)

5 Send an international telegram to a member of your family living abroad telling him or her that your brother has been badly injured in a car accident. Include details of names and addresses of both sender and recipient. You should not exceed 30 words including addresses.

(10 marks)

Send a follow-up letter giving more details and reassuring them that he is out of danger.

(10 marks)

6 Your firm recently carried out a test run of a new product (specify). Prepare a report to be sent from the marketing manager to the board of directors explaining how the test went.

Public very interested in product - sales good - letters already received from other areas of country showing interest - national advertising campaign to be organised (give some details).

(20 marks)

7 An international singing star Ami Paris is to appear in concert in Letford. You have been asked to prepare the material which is to appear on the programme. This is limited to 60 words. Write your passage using the details given below.

Ami was born in Nashville in 1961 and had her first hit record at the age of 15. Most of her work has been done at Gospel Concerts but in 1985 she made it to the top of the American Charts with the song 'One More Song'. In 1984 she married John Pope who has written a number of new hit songs. Last year her first child, Tanya Marie was born. Although her style is rock gospel she can also sing much quieter material to full advantage. Her records are bought by all ages and she has now topped the charts in Australia, America, UK, Jamaica and Canada. In 1985 she had three hit songs in the UK charts at one time. Ami comes from a large family of three brothers and two sisters. Her childhood was a happy one revolving round the church where her father was the minister. Her 1988 UK tour is to take in Letford, Leeds, Luton, Northampton, Birmingham and will culminate in a concert in the Albert Hall on 1 May.

(20 marks)

Worked solutions 1

OXFAM - BANBURY ROAD OXFORD OX5 6YH

Telephone: (0753) 38693

Dear Friend

Please allow me to take just a minute of your time to explain how you could provide very real help to stop the suffering in Ethiopia.

You have probably heard of the famine caused by another year of drought which has deprived millions of hard-working farming people of the crops they depend on for survival. The famine has caused thousands of families to become refugees as homes are abandoned in the search for food and water.

OXFAM is helping in a real way, by providing food and medicine to the suffering, and by helping engineering projects that will bring water to the country's farms.

But OXFAM cannot act alone. It can only help with the support of millions of ordinary people, whose compassion and generosity is moved by the terrible plight of Ethiopia.

Your contribution does not need to be big. £5.00, the price of a paperback book, can bring medicine and blankets to three suffering children.

Please help OXFAM to help Ethiopia. Without your support, we are absolutely powerless to act. But with your support, we can bring relief to thousands of innocent people.

I will close by expressing the deep gratitude of everybody at OXFAM for your help.

Yours sincerely

Malcolm Field

Malcolm Field
Aid Co-ordinator

Commentary

1 The letter is organised and sequenced carefully by paragraph. The opening paragraph is purely introductory, with the second paragraph developing and illustrating the gravity of the famine. The third paragraph explains the role Oxfam takes in helping, while the next three paragraphs all deal concisely with the nature of the help that can be given by donors. The final paragraph provides a courteous conclusion.

2 The impact of the letter is strengthened by the succession of short paragraphs, all of which contribute to the 'readability' of the letter.

3 The letter uses carefully controlled tone. While it asks for money, it does so tactfully, and with particular stress on the effectiveness of relatively small contributions. The reference to 'the price of a paperback book' effectively contrasts the position of people in a wealthy nation with those in a poor one.

2

REPORT ON YOUNG EMPLOYEES' CONDITIONS AT SEAMWELL GARMENTS LTD

A/
TERMS OF REFERENCE:

To produce a report for the Managing Director on the pay and working conditions of young employees, with recommendations.

B/
PROCEDURE:

Three weeks was spent in close observation of the work environment of eighteen of our younger employees.

C/
FINDINGS:

1. The younger employees all use modern equipment, but work in surroundings that are both noisy and cramped. The main workshop area suffers from high noise levels, partly due to the absence of acoustic panels in the roof. The workshop was initially designed for twenty machines, and currently contains twenty-seven.

2. The younger employees are all working to apprentice machinists' levels of pay of £2.25 per hour. This compares with the rate for a qualified machinist of £2.95, a substantial difference. The lower pay level leads to very high amounts of overtime work. Some juniors are working in excess of 60 hours per week.

3. Apprentice machinists can only progress to higher rates if they gain a full Machinist's Certificate of Competence, by attending the local technical college evening class. Many do not do this, because of overtime work. The ability of many of our machinists is not developing as it should.

4. Meal breaks of forty minutes per lunchtime and ten minute tea breaks, morning and afternoon, are very brief. It is unlikely that machinists have sufficient time to fully relax and gather energies for the next session.

5. Since the closure of a hot meals facility last year, the canteen has provided only sandwiches. These are of a good standard and very inexpensive.

6. First aid and rest facilities are very good and well up to standard.

7. The firm currently offers no sports facilities as the staff numbers are too low. However, we have been offered shared use of swimming and sports facilities, including a social club, bar and gymnasium, at the neighbouring plastics factory. Costs would be negotiable.

7. The firm's free bus service from the centre of town works well and is used by all junior employees.

D/
CONCLUSIONS:

Some aspects of our provision for junior employees are of a high standard. These include transport, first aid and rest facilities.

Other facilities are well below standard, and should be immediately improved if we want to keep our younger workers. The facilities that need improvement are as follows:

1. Workshop noise control
2. Poor apprentice pay levels
3. Length of meal and tea breaks
4. Range of canteen food
5. Sports facilities

E/
RECOMMENDATIONS:

1. The firm should immediately instal acoustic panels in its workshop.

2. Apprentice pay should be increased by 25%. Apprentices should be encouraged to attend local evening classes by the company paying course fees.

3. The lunch break should be extended to one hour. Tea breaks should be fifteen rather than ten minutes.

4. The canteen should provide at least one hot dish each day, in addition to sandwiches.

5. The company should take out associate membership of the sports club belonging to the local plastics factory, and should give all employees trial membership for three months.

R Pallett   Personnel Officer   7 June 19-

Commentary

1 The report is carefully organised and sectioned.

2 Language is formal and unemotional.

3 Conclusions and recommendations are carefully distinguished.

4 Lettering and numbering systems are used for headings and sub points to avoid confusion.

3

TO HEAD OFFICE, RIPLON LTD

   TRIP HIGHLY SUCCESSFUL. GAINED SEVEN BUYERS. REQUEST PERMISSION TO STAY UNTIL 25.5.-, AND FOR AN ASSISTANT TO JOIN ME. YEN REVALUATION AND REDUCED IMPORT CONTROLS GIVE EVEN GREATER SCOPE FOR SALES ON CURRENT TRIP. PLEASE ADVISE URGENTLY.
   PALING - HOTEL FUJI - TOKYO.   11.5.-

```
                                          Fuji Hotel
                                          Pacific Prospect
                                          Tokyo 347543

                                          Tel: 4586 258635
                                          Telex: 34587 FUJI
```

Mr I Bell
Sales Director
Riplon Ltd (Head Office)
55 Berkely Square
London W1

Dear Mr Bell

                    SALES TRIP TO JAPAN

I am writing in support of my telegram earlier today, to request a two-week extension of my presence here.

Since my arrival at the beginning of the month, I have found an excellent market for our products, and confirmed sales have already exceeded expectations by a factor of thirty per cent.

I have also found that there is to be a major trade exhibition at this hotel from 20-23 of this month, which will be attended by companies from all over the Pacific region. I am sure we could do extremely well at this exhibition, (where we have been offered a stand) particularly if you could release another member of sales staff to join me here.

A further point is the significant revaluation of the yen, which makes it less expensive for Japanese companies to buy our products, and the reduction of import controls.

In summary, I feel that current conditions are perfect for a further sales presence here and hope that you will agree to my suggestions.

Yours sincerely

Martin Paling

Martin Paling
Sales Manager

Commentary

1 The telegram is brief but perfectly clear in introducing the necessary points.

2 The supporting letter is sufficiently detailed to provide the necessary development and support of the suggestions made in the telegram.

3 The supporting letter closes by requesting a reply, and this virtually guarantees a response.

4

The King's School
Beech Lane
Gloucester GL7 4RG

The Booking Office
Royal Shakespeare Company
Stratford upon Avon
WARWICKSHIRE

Our ref: FB/DHT

Dear Sir

<u>SUMMER SEASON 19-</u>

We are a school with an extremely strong commitment to the study of Shakespeare, and have supported your summer productions for several years.

We would like to reserve tickets for the week of 16-21 July, when a party of eighteen pupils accompanied by two teachers will be staying in a youth hostel in the Stratford area, following the end of school examination season.

As we will be present for a week, the trip offers a unique opportunity to our pupils to see several Shakespeare plays performed.

I am therefore writing to ask if you would be able to provide us with a set of twenty tickets for each of the performances listed below:

16 July: The Merchant of Venice (matinee)
17 July: Cymbeline (matinee)
18 July: Hamlet (matinee)
19 July: Macbeth (matinee)

We are unable to attend evening performances, due to the closure of the Youth Hostel at 10.30pm each night.

I would be most grateful if you could notify me of the availability of tickets. Naturally we will be happy to accept bookings for some of the plays, if it is not possible to accomodate us for all. Our budget enables us to pay up to £6.00 per ticket per performance.

I very much look forward to hearing from you.

Yours sincerely

F Bacon

F Bacon
Head of Drama

Commentary

1 The letter opens with an explanation of the importance of Shakespeare in the school. This serves to explain and strengthen the letter's request for tickets.

2 The letter uses layout very carefully to specify performance details and the particular plays requested.

3 The letter is courteous and professional in tone.

4 The letter provides all necessary details.

5

MEMORANDUM

To: SALES ROOM STAFF   **Date:** 15 July 19-

From: Chief Accountant

Subject: Delivery of Advice Notes and Despatch Notes

The prompt and accurate production of accounts depends on the flow of advice notes and despatch notes into the Accounts Department.

I am therefore writing to ask you to provide such notes as promptly as possible and certainly on the same day as they are produced.

I realise that you are under considerable pressure of work, but a speedy flow of despatch notes and advice notes will be of enormous help to us.

Sharon Leeds   Chief Accountant

Commentary

1 The memo is brief and concise.

2 The memo fully explains the purpose of the request.

3 The memo recognises the difficulty under which recipients work, but outlines the advantages of the change it requests.

4 The memo is clear and courteous, while avoiding formality which would be unnecessary in an internal communication.

6

55 Downbank Avenue
Bridgend
Mid Glamorgan   CF1 5RT

R J Williams
Company Secretary
John Pollard and Sons plc
Industrial Estate
Bridgend
Glamorgan   CF4 2DF

8 March 19—

Dear Mr Williams

<u>TRAINEE PERSONNEL OFFICER</u>

I am writing in response to your advertisement for a trainee Personnel Officer, which appeared in <u>The Bridgend Herald</u> on the fourth of this month.

I left Bridgend School in June last year, having gained GCSE passes in English Language, Mathematics, Art, Biology and French. Since this time I have worked as an assistant interviewer with Jameson and Co, a market research firm in Cardiff.

I have enjoyed this work, but would now like to build on the experience of working with people by undertaking personnel work with an established company such as yourselves. I am particularly interested in the personnel aspects of women working in industry. I would therefore be most interested in working for Pollard and Sons, as I believe you have an unusually large proportion of women in senior management positions.

I very much hope to hear from you, and to meet you at interview. My referees are as follows:

Mrs H Jones, Headteacher, Bridgend School, Bridgend, CF 3RT 5GJ. Tel: (6534) 36853.

Mr Malcolm Prior, Senior Research Manager, Jameson and Co, 345 Rhonnda Drive, Cardiff CO11 4VJ. Tel: (0456) 58613.

Yours sincerely

Caroline Moores

Caroline Moores

Commentary

1 The letter provides all necessary details of a letter of application, including educational background, work background, referees, and the source of the advertisement for the vacancy.

2 However, the main strength of this letter is that it presents the candidate's personal and individual reasons for applying for the vacancy, in a clear, concise and convincing manner.

Advanced examination questions 131

7

INSTRUCTIONS FOR THE USE OF THE PHOTOCOPIER

1. Before operation, please check the following points:

i) That the copier is plugged in to the main wall power socket.

ii) That the copier main switch (on the top right-hand edge of the copier surface) is on, and that the red light next to the switch is glowing. This shows that the power is on.

iii) That the paper tray, at the left-hand side of the copier, made of black plastic, contains paper. The copier uses only one size of paper – A4. Paper is stored in the cupboard beneath the copier.

iv) That the warning light next to the red power light is off. If this light is on, the copier needs attention. Please alert the Office Manager if this is the case.

You are now ready to copy.

2. Take the original document. Lift the yellow flap on top of the copier, and place the original document face down on the glass, with the upper right-hand corner of the document placed against the arrow at the corner of the glass.

3. Close the yellow flap.

4. Set the dial to show the number of copies you require (any number from 1 to 20).

5. Press the green PRINT button at the side of the copier.

6. Wait until the copier stops movement before removing your copies.

If there is any difficulty, please consult the Office Manager.

Commentary

1 The instructions are clear and simple.

2 The instructions distinguish controls by reference to their colour and position on the copier.

3 The instructions are divided helpfully into two sections: procedures to prepare for copying, and procedures for copying.

4 The instructions do not become too complicated, but illustrate basic procedures only.

31 Preparing for examinations

You should now have developed the necessary skills in business communication to enable you to complete successfully the PEI examinations in English for Business Communication at all levels. To complement and finalise what you have learned you must now focus specifically on the techniques necessary to **prepare for** and **complete** the examination successfully. Many students encounter particular difficulty with the examination, and cannot easily reproduce the quality of their coursework under examination conditions. This section is therefore divided into three sections:
- Preparing for a PEI examination
- Examination technique in a PEI examination
- What examiners look for

Preparing for a PEI examination

Many students fail examinations, not because they lack the necessary knowledge and skills, but because they have not prepared for the examination with sufficient method and care. This may be the case even if the student has spent many hours revising: such hours are often underused or even wasted because of certain common faults in examination preparation.

Common faults in examination preparation

- insufficient time spent revising
- revision is done on the basis of inadequate material (for example, incomplete notes and incomplete sample exercises)
- preparation is undertaken without a careful analysis of syllabus topics, and without identifying individual strengths and weaknesses
- insufficient practice at **timed writing**, in examination conditions
- insufficient study of past examination papers

Apart from the first fault listed, all the other faults are remedied by careful **planning** of revision. Remember that your revision process is designed to **identify** and **strengthen** any weaknesses in your ability to manage the syllabus. This does not mean that the revision process will eliminate difficulties that have arisen during a particular course of study, but it does mean that you will gain an awareness of your strengths and weaknesses throughout the syllabus as a whole. This will give you two advantages:
1 It will enable detailed revision to concentrate on the reduction of your weaknesses.
2 It may enable you to conduct revision selectively so that areas of weakness, once identified, are avoided in the examination paper. (This is likely to be a useful strategy in the advanced examination, where the presence of optional questions make it possible for candidates to avoid entire question areas.)

How to prepare yourself for a PEI examination

1 Make a syllabus topic list. An example is shown on the following pages for each of the three levels of PEI examination.)

2 Classify each topic as:
A **strength** – a topic which you have fully learned, which you feel competent and confident to perform in the examination, and which needs little revision.
A **competence** – a topic which you have studied, but which you have not found easy, although you have basically grasped and understood it. With a little careful revision and some practice questions, you can polish your performance up to a satisfactory examination standard.
A **weakness** – a topic about which you remain unhappy, despite careful study and frequent practice. Topics of the last type will need careful revision and repeated practice. If they are optional questions, you may choose to avoid them in the examination. This classification is best done by reviewing your past performance on individual exam topics.

3 Organise your revision time by allocating **priority** to those topics which are either weaknesses, or which remain only at the level of a competence. Once you have noted these on your planner as a high priority, you will remember to allocate suitable amounts of time to each topic.

If you have completed the checklist at the beginning of each part of this guide you will find that you have a detailed guide to your strengths, competences and weaknesses.

4 Revise methodically, over a suitable period of time. Remember that:
Revision time is most efficient when split into units of between 45 and 90 minutes. Do not study for more than 90 minutes without a break, or your concentration and revision quality will decline.
The most effective **timing** for successful revision is from *six* weeks **before an examination** to *one* week before an examination. The bulk of your systematic, topic by topic revision should be done in this time. The final week should be spent selectively, on two or three problem topics, and should not be so intense as to cause you to enter the examination jaded or tired.
Your revision must include **timed** writing of PEI past examination questions.

Syllabus topic list: English for Business Communication

Elementary

Topic	Classification (Str/Comp/Weak)	Priority (High/Med/Low)	Revision complete (Tick)
Reading/Vocabulary			
Letter			
Memorandum			
Telex			
International Telegram			

Intermediate

Topic	Classification	Priority	Revision complete
Letter from notes on business matter			
Compulsory report (from information given)			
Memorandum from brief notes			
International telegram and confirming letter			
Telephone messages			
Personal letter, reply to invitation			
Business letter (simpler than compulsory question)			
Report (shorter than compulsory report)			

Preparing for examinations 135

Advanced

Topic	Classification (Str/Comp/Weak)	Priority (High/Med/Low)	Revision complete (Tick)
Compulsory letter (business)			
Compulsory report (formal)			
Compulsory telegram, notice, advertisement or other concise text			
Memorandum			
Personal letter			
Report on event or events, or series of correspondence			
Extracting points from continuous prose (summary)			

Examination technique

Examination candidates frequently perform below their full potential in examinations. This is often because of poor examination technique. Examination technique means simply the ability to perform efficiently under the limited activities and times of a formal examination. The following suggestions can help to improve examination technique.

1 As an examination is a test of your ability to perform under constraints of time, practice regularly before the examination in writing answers to examination questions under timed conditions.

2 Develop the habit of reading examination questions, and all instructions to candidates with particular care. Examination marks are frequently wasted by candidates who answer the wrong questions, or who answer in the wrong way.

3 Read through the paper carefully before you begin. Select the questions that you will answer. If you feel that you are unlikely to score well on one particular question, leave it until last. Try to maximise your marks by dealing fully and firstly with those questions on which you feel confident and assured.

4 Work out the total time available, and allocate a time limit to each question you tackle. This will increase your chances of scoring well on each question, and avoid the possibility of spending too much time on individual questions, at the expense of others.

5 Leave five minutes at the end to check over work, and to neatly rule through any rough work.

6 Use a type of pen with which you are familiar and comfortable, and ensure you that you have a second pen in reserve.

What examiners look for

Examination candidates often wish they knew their examiners, and had some idea of what examiners are looking for, and what they are likely to reward and/or penalise.

This can be done quite easily, by studying **past PEI papers** in conjunction with a recent **PEI examiners' report**. This is an account of the examiners' views on the responses given by candidates in a particular syllabus. The reports detail the approaches and skills which examiners look for.

In general, all questions at every level should show an understanding of **layout**, **content**, **expression** and **style**.

In PEI Examinations, the layout of particular forms of written communication should display the following aspects:-

Letters	*Reports*	*Memoranda*
Address	Terms of Reference	To
Addressee	Heading	From
Reference	Date	Subject Heading
Date	Signature	Signature
Salutation	Headings	Date
Heading	Sub headings and/or	Reference
Subscription	numbered sections or	
Signature	sub sections.	
Enclosures (if any)	Conclusions	
	Recommendations	
	(if any)	

At advanced level, the layout of documents should be similar to that adopted at Intermediate level. It is important to remember that examiners at Advanced level always look to see the candidate's ability to **develop** the material given in the questions.

Examiners' reports

General comments

It would appear that some Centres are entering candidates for the Advanced level before they are ready to sit the examination, or otherwise they are not being properly taught to the higher level.

Areas of good performance

Part 1 of the Elementary level is generally very well answered with candidates frequently obtaining full marks. Business letters are generally well answered.

Candidates must learn to read questions very carefully and try to give an answer which is appropriate, avoiding meaningless information.

At Advanced level, candidates who are passing are generally performing well and show an ability to give additional information such as addresses, dates and prices when required.

Also available in this series:

PEI Guide to Word Processing
by Annetta Perry

The PEI Guide to Word Processing offers practice and support for candidates preparing for Pitman elementary and intermediate word processing examinations. Like the examinations, it is not limited to specific software but offers complete coverage of the essential elements of word processing at both levels.

Published by Pitman for Pitman examinations, this top quality study and revision textbook is without parallel.

Published 1990, 224 pages, ISBN 0 273 03201 1